Peter Fleming (1907–71) was a jou
one of the last great adventurers of th
began his career as a special corres
and later wrote for *The Spectator* fo
career as a journalist. He served with the Grenadier Guards
during World War II and from 1942 was in charge of military
deception operations in Southeast Asia. He is author of
several classic books, which include *Brazilian Adventure,
One's Company, News from Tartary, Bayonets to Lhasa* and
A Forgotten Journey, published here as *To Peking*. In his
memory, the Royal Geographical Society established the
Peter Fleming Award for projects that seek to advance
geographical science.

Praise for Peter Fleming

Brazilian Adventure

'The best travel book I have read for a long time. It is crammed with sound observation, good writing, humour and a unique blend of disillusion, foolhardiness and high spirits.'

J. B. Priestley

'This account of the expedition has that essential double interest which is characteristic of all really great books of adventure. Mr. Fleming has the most delightful sense of humour and he writes brilliantly.'   David Garnett

One's Company

'Original and impressive . . . As a journalist he is modernity itself; as a traveller he has about him an Elizabethan aroma, being both cruel and amused.'

Harold Nicolson, *Daily Telegraph*

'A classic traveller.'   Compton Mackenzie, *Daily Mail*

'With an acid and scornful mind, a fresh and vivid style . . . One reads him for literary delight and for the pleasure of meeting an Elizabethan spirit allied to a modern mind . . . but he is also an observer of penetrating intellect.'

Vita Sackville-West, *The Spectator*

News from Tartary

'Its entertainment value is immense. It will arouse great fury and cause much pleasure.'   Harold Nicolson

'It confirmed Fleming's place in the front rank of travel writers . . . no modern work of travel has given me more pleasure . . . I have read it more times than I can remember.'

Nigel Buxton

'Mr. Fleming will be remembered as a gifted writer with an easy pen given to satire . . . This kind of journey and this kind of book are at his fingertips.'   V. S. Pritchett

'A simple blending of modesty and wit in disarming proportions . . . the result is something fresh and delightful in the literature of high Asia.'   *New York Times*

'One of the most impressive volumes that has come from Asia in many years . . . unadulterated reporting . . . brilliantly written and candidly truthful.'

G. E. Sokolsky, *Saturday Review of Literature*

'I read the book for the pleasure of Mr. Fleming's company. Like thousands of other people I am charmed by his highly impudent street-urchin approach to danger and discomfort, to hunger and thirst.'   David Garnett, *New Statesman*

The Siege at Peking

'An exceptionally readable book.'   *Sunday Times*

'an astonishing tale . . . exciting, enthralling, at times humorous and always strictly accurate, this is a thoroughly enjoyable book.'   *Time and Tide*

To Peking

'Peter Fleming's *To Peking* tells the story of a long journey, with much that is relevant for us to-day, From the Caucasus to Shanghai, via Tashkent, Irkutz and Valdivostok, Fleming sharpens his keen eye and caustic wit on bewitching places and a medley of colourful characters he encounters along the way. Written with the immediacy of a diary, this is not a journey the reader will easily forget.'

John Hare, author of *Mysteries of the Gobi*

Tauris Parke Paperbacks is an imprint of I.B.Tauris. It is dedicated to publishing books in accessible paperback editions for the serious general reader within a wide range of categories, including biography, history, travel and the ancient world. The list includes select, critically acclaimed works of top quality writing by distinguished authors that continue to challenge, to inform and to inspire. These are books that possess those subtle but intrinsic elements that mark them out as something exceptional.

The Colophon of Tauris Parke Paperbacks is a representation of the ancient Egyptian ibis, sacred to the god Thoth, who was himself often depicted in the form of this most elegant of birds. Thoth was credited in antiquity as the scribe of the ancient Egyptian gods and as the inventor of writing and was associated with many aspects of wisdom and learning.

TO PEKING

A Forgotten Journey from Moscow to Manchuria

Peter Fleming

Foreword by
Simon Winchester

TAURIS PARKE
PAPERBACKS

Published in 2009 by Tauris Parke Paperbacks
An imprint of I.B.Tauris and Co Ltd
6 Salem Road, London W2 4BU
175 Fifth Avenue, New York NY 10010
www.ibtauris.com

Distributed in the United States and Canada Exclusively by
Palgrave Macmillan
175 Fifth Avenue, New York NY 10010

First published as *A Forgotten Journey* by Rupert Hart-Davis in 1952

ISBN: 978 1 84511 996 6

A full CIP record for this book is available from the British Library
A full CIP record is available from the Library of Congress

Library of Congress Catalog Card Number: available

Printed and bound in India by Thomson Press India Ltd

CONTENTS

ILLUSTRATIONS

TO PEKING

Though outgunned in the marketplace by his younger brother Ian, birth-father of James Bond, the literary laurels of the remarkable Oxfordshire banker-family Fleming go without doubt or demur to Peter, who from his upbringing in Mayfair to his death in Argyll lived a life of gilded adventuring about which, to the delight of millions, he wrote without cease.

Though he wandered widely he was most fascinated by what it was once permissible to call 'The East.' The amused detachment with which he described events and places he encountered between the Urals and the China Sea that he found by turns thrilling, dangerous and generally utterly unknown, and the witheringly accurate judgments that he rendered on the bounders, savages and capital fellows he met *en route*, have become the stuff of a classic, if archly dated, style of travel writing. Those who still like the robust storytelling of Kipling and John Buchan and Patrick Leigh Fermor always adored Peter Fleming; today's readers of a more sensitive and politically correct persuasion might yet find him a little rich for their taste. For these, *To Peking* may prove an unsuspected charmer.

This small book, to all intents and purposes an annotated diary, lay forgotten in a drawer in Merrimoles, Oxfordshire, where Fleming settled in 1945 with his wife, the celebrated actress Celia Johnson. He had written it in 1934, while he was travelling eastwards from Russia to Manchuria on a wide-ranging commission for *The Times*.

It was his second such expedition for what was then Britain's most esteemed newspaper; the first, made in 1933, just four years after his coming down from Christ Church (where, after Eton, he had taken a first in English) had settled his reputation as the exemplar of the foreign correspondent—a romantic, up-for-anything wanderer whose exploits (despite being written anonymously) brought both wry and knowing amusement to the breakfast-tables and the drawing rooms of the Establishment, as well as admiring gossip to the smoking rooms of the better Pall Mall clubs.

Already he had achieved a precocious literary success: *Brazilian Adventure*, a rollicking account of his ill-advised attempt (made when he was twenty-five) to find the missing explorer Colonel Fawcett, had been a minor triumph both in Britain and America; and his first journalistic foray into war-ravaged China a year later provided him with material for an equally memorable volume, *One's Company*, which showed him as infinitely resourceful, impeccably connected and hugely brave—as well as irrepressibly funny.

This 1934 diary, written on a portable typewriter (and illustrated with the use of his faithful old Leica III camera) records his thoughts and observations during an odyssey that took him from Moscow, initially through the Caucasus—skirting what are now Chechnya and South Ossetia, both as thick with guns then as today—and on eastward by way of Central Asia to Siberia's Lake Baikal, to what was then the Japanese puppet state of Manchukuo, and finally into China proper. Throughout his road and railway meanderings Fleming maintains a sturdily patrician view of those around him, a wry amusement at the curious doings of foreigners, and what those tolerant of his manner might describe as a teasing sense of play.

On almost every page there is material calculated,

amiably, to offend. Here he is, for example, describing his Caucasus interpreter and companion, Boris: "a swarthy, seedy, shifty-looking man who claims to have been at Oxford (though his college— St. Catherine's—does not in my opinion exist)." Whatever Boris himself might think of that, graduates of St. Catherine's might well take issue— until realising that Fleming is merely stating the obvious, a commentary on himself: that to his circle of swells a college that was in those days as socially undesirable as it was unfashionable might as well never have been built.

It is perhaps the more casual observations that offer up the greatest pleasure. As when he travels in a Georgian train "with three men who grossly underestimated the value of ventilation." Or when, returning tipsy from a late-night *ceilidh* in some godforsaken village nearby, "I did a creditable bit of path-finding back to the hotel, passing on the way two men of a very cheerful kind who were settling down for the night in a municipal dustbin." And again: "At 3.30 my train arrives and an imbecile railway official puts me in the wrong carriage. I have to sleep on the narrow shelf intended for luggage and backed by the hot water pipes. I have some tinned things but no liquids of any kind. The carriage is crammed with dreary women and seedy Chinese. In the morning everyone is rather disagreeable."

On occasion seriousness and prescience obtrude. Sometimes the seriousness is favourable: as when Fleming arrives in Mukden—today's Shenyang—to find he had been offered the editorship of the *Observer* (he turned it down). Sometimes it is less so: "I discover that my despatch case is gone. I ask the manager, Medvedev, if he will take a cheque. He says no. There is a good deal of coldness."

And hints of prescience are everywhere. He has little time, for example, for the militaristic Japanese he encounters in what was once Chinese Manchuria; and when he hears that a party of troopers have made themselves offensive to his friend the great Swiss traveler Ella Maillart (who would later go on to journey from Peking to Srinagar in company with Fleming, each of the pair later producing classic accounts of the adventure) he exclaimed in a footnote: "It was not difficult, as one travelled in the back parts of Manchuria, to sense in the Japanese soldiery a latent desire to ill-treat and humiliate members of the white races. I always thought this repressed urge would break out, given a favourable opportunity..." As, of course, it later did—in Bataan, in Changi, on the River Kwai railway...

Most of all the charm of this slender volume resides in its writing. It has, like all great diaries, that clarity of vision that is occasioned by the hastiness of record. Since it is all so elegantly written by an observer of great wisdom and learning, then—providing that the reader accepts the aristocratic, vaguely imperial and long-outmoded tone, which renders the volume as much a portrait of Peter Fleming as of the countryside through which he ventures—it is a document almost entirely pleasurable to read. As, taken in this vein, is just about everything that Peter Fleming ever wrote.

When he died at sixty-four years old, on a shooting holiday in his beloved western Scotland in the late summer of 1971—a death, said his obituarist, that was "exactly as he would have chosen"—his body was brought home to Oxfordshire. Celia Johnson, who outlived him by more than a decade, saw to it that his tombstone was then suitably engraved, and thus his memorial remains today:

> *He travelled widely in far places:*
> *Wrote, and was widely read.*
> *Soldiered, saw some of danger's faces.*
> *Came home to Nettlebed.*
>
> *The squire lies here, his journeys ended.*
> *Dust, and a name on a stone.*

Content, amid the lands he tended,
To keep this rendezvous alone.

———————————

Simon Winchester

PREFACE

In August 1934 I left England for the Far East, with the ultimate intention (which I did not really expect to be able to carry out) of returning from China to India by an overland route through Central Asia. It was my third journey to China, and I travelled as a Special Correspondent of *The Times*. I was twenty-seven years old.

It was not until February of the following year that I came, so to speak, under starter's orders for the Central Asian enterprise, whose long course and lucky outcome are described in *News from Tartary*. In the intervening five months I had covered, in a desultory sort of way, a good deal of ground in regions some of which can fairly be described as out of the way and to all of which access is, for a Western traveller, now no longer possible. During these months, besides sending home a series of despatches to *The Times*, I kept a diary; and it is of that diary that this book consists.

The entries were typed, often under inconvenient conditions, into a loose-leaf notebook. I came across it the other day and read it through for the first time for more than fifteen years. One is always interested in an account of one's own experiences, especially if—as in this case—the experiences themselves have long lain neglected in the box-room of one's memory; but it is hardly the sort of interest which one can expect others to share. I wished that at the time the wanderings of

13

those five months had not been overshadowed by the more difficult and more purposeful journey to whose jumping-off point they brought me, and that I had written a book about them.

Then I began to wonder whether the diary might not be worth publishing as it stood. Slapdash, superficial, and often obscure, it is very far from the urbane tradition of the *carnets de voyage;* but it does provide, here and there, a glimpse of peoples and places which the present generation are not likely to be able to see for themselves, and its inconsequent entries do partly recapture the atmosphere of more spacious days, of a freer world in which Tiflis and Tashkent, Vladivostok and Harbin were not forbidden destinations. I re-read the loose-leaf notebook and decided to publish its contents, together with some of the photographs which I took at the time.

I have called the result *A Forgotten Journey* because I really had forgotten—as far as details are concerned—almost everything about the events of those five months until the diary refreshed my memory; and even now I remember them only imperfectly—far too imperfectly to recast the material into a more polished and coherent form without some sacrifice of honesty and some risk to truth. In the pages which follow I have made only the following departures from or additions to the original text:

(a) I have added short footnotes, or shorter explanations in square brackets, wherever they seemed necessary or desirable.

(b) I have deleted various passages containing data—probably inaccurate then and wholly incomprehensible now—about such matters as troop movements, opium prices, and railway construction.

(c) I have replaced abbreviations and initials by the names of the organisations or individuals which they represented—e.g. "South Manchurian Railway" instead of S.M.R.

(d) I have omitted a few purely personal entries, all very short and almost all irrelevant to the events I was recording.

In no other respects do the contents of this book differ from those of the loose-leaf notebook upon whose first page, after my name, is prudently if perhaps rather sanguinely typed the injunction:

"Please return to
British Embassy,
Moscow—
British Legation,
Peking—
or Nettlebed,
Oxon
(whichever is nearest)."

Nettlebed, 1952   PETER FLEMING

FIRST STAGE

TO MOSCOW

TO MOSCOW

[The first part of the journey was undertaken in the company of Lord and Lady Gage. Our object was to try and get some shooting in the Caucasus. They would thereafter take passage in a tanker across the Black Sea and return to England; I hoped to get permission to continue my journey to Manchuria by the shortest route—across the Caspian Sea and up the Turksib Railway through Russian Central Asia to its junction with the Trans-Siberian Railway.]

AUGUST 29, 1934. (In Poland.)

Left on Aug. 27. Plethora of bowler hats at Liverpool Street softened the wrench. Journey to Berlin with the Gages laconic, uneventful, agreeable. Exchange lousy. It always is. On the boat the same sun, the same caparisoned hikers, the same fish for lunch, and the same self-disgust [1] as last year. Holland no less flat.

Berlin. Took a communal bathroom at the Adlon, than which I know of no more depressing hotel. Empty, dark, pompous. The early office-goers in the Linden seemed to me a trifle haunted; but perhaps that was only their dyspepsia, or mine, We called on Bulgey

[1] The diarist's reasons for being disgusted with himself, though doubtless sound enough, have been forgotten.

Thorne,[1] who seemed to me very courteous and very able. The usual tabloid summary of the German situation, during which I heard for the first time of their former military liaison with the Red Army. Then a polite visit to a museum; I searched pictures for oddities and drama and nothing else. We lunched with a young Bismarck, very highly civilised, charming, expressing a pleasant lackadaisical despair. He lives in Rome and I imagine dilettants. He was very kind to us, though clearly loathing it, and in the afternoon George and Mogs [Gage] went with him to Potsdam in the pouring rain—it rained all day—and saw Labour Corps doing arms drill with spades and other wonders.

I went and saw Reed,[2] the *Times* man, who was nice, is said to be able, and emanated a slightly Printing House Square atmosphere. He said Goebbels would be the first of the top-line maniacs to go, since he makes himself so hated, and told me a story of Jews near Frankfurt being sympathetic to Hitler. Thence I went to Knickerbocker,[3] whom I found among his suitcases with his wife—very like an American foreign correspondent's wife—and his publisher, an intensely jovial German. They were pleasant, and he told me that he is going to Manchuria. After that I fiddled about writing and wiring and telephoning till seven, when we all went to a film called *Maskerade*, with a new Viennese actress

[1] Lt.-Gen. Sir Andrew Thorne, K.C.B., C.M.G., D.S.O., was at that time our Military Attaché in Berlin.

[2] Mr. Douglas Reed. Three years later, in Vienna, he told me the story of his life. I suggested that he ought to write a book about it and gave him a letter of introduction to my publisher. The result was *Insanity Fair*.

[3] Mr. H. R. Knickerbocker, a very likeable person, was killed in an air crash in India in 1949.

called Paula Wessely, who was fairly ugly and nothing extra. But the film was a good job of high comedy. We could only get three seats, so the hapless Bismarck had to go home. He must have had a terrible day.

Afterwards we ate Frankfurters in a café and then spent hours at the station fiddling about with our luggage. I recommended taking almost everything in our sleepers, for cheapness and security, but was nearly forestalled by an official who objected that we had more than was allowed and must register more. We had hardly any marks, so this looked bad. But I suggested that George should proclaim himself, and at the sight of his *laissez-passer* [1] snobbery triumphed and we got away with it. Mogs sat on the luggage and read *War and Peace* unperturbed.

The train is quite empty, and the customs invasion at the Polish frontier in the middle of the night was not a serious one; we had hidden our money, in case. The only other foreigner on the train is a dim Shanghai-lander (14 years there) called G——. He has rheumatism and looks typical. He is going right through. The conductor is charming. He gave us two English books which a passenger had left with him on entering Russia. One of them was *The Intelligent Man's Guide Through World Chaos*. It seems a silly thing to leave behind on the Russian frontier. I have been reading the Caucasus guide-book. There are some good bits. "The mountain horses are very prudent." "The Soviet has instituted civil marriage, etc." Also some fine fauna, headed by the white field-rat.

[1] George, who was at that time a Lord in Waiting to King George V, had been given by the German Foreign Office a document asking officials to treat him with courtesy and consideration.

The usual Polish breakfast of cheese and ham and chemical honey, and I am shirking lunch. The quest for black roubles hasn't yet been successful The customs at Niegoreloje were worse than heretofore. Nobody spoke more than two words of anything but Russian, and I had a bloody man whom I made to hate me by laughing at him.He opened everything, found none of the tobacco or things he was supposed to be looking for, and finally gave it up in disgust. The porters as usual were feckless and irresolute, and I carried all my luggage on to the train, which was crowded for once. The radio was playing excruciating music in all the carriages, but after some guerrilla warfare we silenced ours. Through the conductor, I had bought 800 roubles for £4 at Stolpce; the bulk of these crossed the frontier in my sock and will be a godsend. George I am afraid is too respectable to smuggle. At Niegoreloje we picked up a team of athletes returning with a vast and hideous piece of silverware from an allegedly victorious contest in Paris. They were feasted at Niegoreloje, and later received with a band, each athlete being hoisted in the air in turn by the enthusiastic crowd. Large bouquets were also presented, and one of these, the supply being greater than the demand, was finally thrust upon George by a posse of dwarf women dressed like canteen workers. He looked bashful and not un-Slav, so I suppose the error was venial. I shared a compartment with the javelin thrower, a charming, handsome, but reticent youth, who slept in his running trunks. I talked till a late hour with a young man attached to the train who spoke fair English and felt his vocation to be that of a "tongue-maker"; he said he was there to make things easier for the foreigners, but of this he was of course quite incapable. The International Luxury Express is pervaded as usual by a thick atmosphere of inefficiency. No eggs for breakfast; the menu written only in practically illegible Russian; doors always being found locked, none can say why.

AUGUST 30

After a long and revealing conversation with the nice, dim G——, during which he read out letters from his children at great length, we reached Moscow, an hour and a half before the scheduled time. On the platform a large military band welcomed the athletes, and a squad of some twelve inexpressibly ugly girls, wearing red caps and tight blue sort of bathing dresses made of silk, presented more bouquets. There were also drawn up two long ranks of cretinous-looking athletes in running kit, and a complete football team, dressed for the field, and headed by an amiable man who looked rather like Roger.[1] There were cheers, speeches, tunes, and finally a grand march past, which left us looking desolately for an Intourist man. One finally appeared, a man of the maximum incompetence; he took our luggage away and lost it. Then came another, rather more on the spot, and he found us a car and went on imploring us to be patient until I went and found the luggage. We then drove, with an irrelevant and silent girl interpreter, through sunny streets, cleaner than before,

[1] Roger Pettiward was, as readers of *Brazilian Adventure* may remember, an admirable person and would, I suspect, have been by now recognised as an artist of great distinction and originality. Unhappily he was killed while leading a particularly gallant attack during the successful operations of No. 4 Commando against German coastal batteries at Dieppe in August 1942.

to the National Hotel, where the Gages are installed in great state and me in comfort. The smell of insecticide is said [1] to be overpowering, and my passport is out of order, the fault of Intourist in London.

Duranty [2] came round at lunch time, as helpful and impressive as ever. He confirmed the *Times* Riga stuff about Nationalism booming in the last three or four months, but wouldn't attribute it all to the Far Eastern situation. He thought Urga impossible, the Turksib not. On the whole prospects are not bright, but I will manage something. [3]

Later we went to the Park of Rest and Culture in a powerful car with a nice intelligent female interpreter. This was a large cheerful place, a kind of austere and purposeful Coney Island. What look like sideshows turn out to be reading rooms. The shrubs are exploited to reproduce the features of Stalin or the Chelyuskin heroes. [4] It was very full, today being the rest day.

[1] I have virtually no sense of smell; hence the reliance on hearsay.

[2] Mr. Walter Duranty, an Englishman by birth, was for many years the correspondent in Moscow of the *New York Times*.

[3] While in the U.S.S.R. I wanted, but did not expect to be allowed, to do two things. One was to travel through Russian Central Asia on the Turkestan–Siberia Railway (the Turksib), which was then more or less out of bounds; the other was to visit the People's Republic of Outer Mongolia, which was completely forbidden. Urga (now known as Ulan Bator) is the capital of this Soviet satellite state, at that time the only one of its kind.

[4] In February 1934 the *Chelyuskin*, a Russian ship on service in the Arctic, was crushed in the ice and sank near Wrangel Island, off the north-eastern coast of Siberia. Her complement, numbering 103 and including several women and children, were marooned on the ice with such stores as they had been able to unload before their ship went down. Their rescue by air, a hazardous business protracted over two months, aroused tremendous excitement in Russia. The names "Chelyuskin" and "Schmidt" (the leader of

Almost everyone looked happy and well—better, on the whole, than a London crowd at the end of the summer. Clothes were mixed, unprepossessing, but respectable. A lot of see-saws, roundabouts, etc., in full swing. We watched an open-air chess festival, timed by a stopwatch; there's nothing like being organised. Six blacks, six whites, made their moves simultaneously. There is a great deal of music in the air at Moscow. Lots of bands, lots of loudspeakers. We watched children unselfconsciously learning to dance in public to the practically inaudible music of a sort of concertina played by an abstracted man in the middle of their ever-widening circle. They were coached by two graceful but perspiring girls. We saw also huge grotesque grinning papiermâché giants exemplifying civic misdemeanours. Here the little boys (their real names were given on a notice) who had picked illicit flowers on the nth of June, there the man who had been caught selling dud gramophones in his shop. In another place cartoons were used as posters in a housing campaign in the same way; the names and addresses of the bad landlords caricatured were prominently displayed. A queer, perhaps effective custom.

We saw also an equestrian display by Red Army cavalry. In the middle of the informal ring a white-shirted officer on a flashy black horse supervised operations. These consisted first of three soldiers who did elementary gymkhana vaulting-into-the-saddle stuff at the canter; then of twelve rather smarter cavalrymen, including three cavalrywomen, who trotted interminably

the marooned party) were bestowed on new streets and buildings in many parts of the Union; and the order of "Hero of the Soviet Union" was specially instituted to reward the pilots concerned in the rescue work.

round the ring on awful screws, and then carried out elementary evolutions in slow time with only a partial success. Above this *manège* hung a banner bearing the words "Welcome to the Dog Show."

There was as a matter of fact a dog show outside the Park. All the posters showed large Alsatian-type animals taking part in the defence of their country. Graphic pictures of trenches, etc. Moreover inside the park there was a decent crowd of all ages round a tank of which soldiers were demonstrating the mechanism. Ditto round a model of the Maxim Gorki, the world's largest propaganda aeroplane;[1] and in the children's section everyone above the age of 10 seemed very airminded.

There was a pleasant atmosphere about the afternoon, which was the nicest I have had in Moscow. The people are very likeable—natural and incurious, like children. On the way back we delivered George's letter at the American Embassy, who gave him a more specific and heartening welcome than the British ditto, who had been somewhat distant over the telephone.

Dined off caviar and some thick red wine, walked round the highly romantic Red Square, started *La Condition Humaine*, and slept like a hog. The Red Square is being set for the Sept. 1 demonstration. The big posters are in 5 languages—Russian, French, German, English, and (oddly) [2] Chinese.

[1] The A.N.T. 15, known as the "Maxim Gorki", was an eight-engined monoplane designed for propaganda work. It carried a printing press, a wireless transmitter, cinematograph apparatus, and various loud-hailer devices. It crashed with the loss of 48 lives in 1935 after a collision with a small aircraft which was accompanying it on a demonstration flight.

[2] Not, as can now be seen, a very well-chosen adverb.

AUGUST 31

Gingered up Intourist about arrangements in the morning, then went with George to VOKS [some sort of cultural organisation], where he had a long, slow housing conversation with a little broken-nosed man who had lived in England and was glib. Our nice interpreter then tried to do some telephoning for me, but without any success. It took for instance 20 minutes to get on to the Foreign Office; and then I was cut off. We walked up to the *Moscow Daily News*, to discover that Borodin [1] was away and to be greeted by a dowdy fair American girl who claimed to have known me in Shanghai in 1931 and spoke highly of the Caucasus. Louis Fischer was at the hotel when I got back, a tough, saturnine, likeable, probably sincere intellectual. The most interesting thing he told me was that the Japs are active in Chinese Turkestan and use Turks, the former Emir Pasha men, enemies of Kemal Pasha. He had seen reports of conversations in Constantinople.[2] He thinks I have a chance of Urga but doubts the Turksib.

[1] The *Moscow Daily News* was published in English, on the assumption—at that time a reasonable one—that there would always be enough English-speaking foreigners in Russia to justify the issue of a daily paper in a language they could understand. The editor, Borodin, of whom Mr. Arthur Ransome gave an interesting and judicious account in *The Chinese Puzzle* (1927), had been the leader of a small but influential Russian Mission to Dr. Sun Yatsen's revolutionary government in Canton in the middle 1920's. He was a prime mover in the introduction of Communism to China. In 1934 he was out of favour with the régime and I never heard of him again.

[2] This information was, to the best of my later knowledge, wholly without foundation. It well typifies the authoritative but chimerical intelligence about remote parts of Asia which one was always picking up.

27

Just back from a 40-days' tour in the country and has never seen it looking better. Ditto Moscow; e.g. you can buy inner tubes for a child's bicycle. Morale high in Army; good spirit and tradition (men make way for women in trams, unlike civilians); top men good, battalion commanders also good; and young. (Cf. Duranty's point that Russia would not have to spend the first six months of a war cutting away dead wood at the top.) Concentrating on mechanisation. Chemical warfare side well advanced; big works in Eastern Siberia. A nice man.

Then we had a conference with the assistant director of Intourist and a Caucasus expert in George's room— the sort of crack that does one good, with a lot of maps and wild names. The plans sound OK to me, indeed very OK; but my chances of the Turksib are not what they might be. It will be a funny journey if it comes off. I did a lot of the Keen Young Sportsman stuff, which may have helped to allay their suspicions.

The hotel is pretty good, and Moscow looks much better than it did.

Duranty and a mixed bag of minor diplomats came in for a drink, and we had the usual vague Moscow party. Thayer, Bullitt's secretary, talked about the polo, which they had convinced Voroshiloff was just what the Red Cavalry needed. They started playing on an enormous plain bounded on three sides by the river, riding enormous stallions. It was difficult to get them to go hard, because they said it was Not Culture. But they were very keen. There was no such thing as the close of play; only the fall of night.

Dined on generalisations, mutely refereed by Mogs.

TO MOSCOW

Woke up early and walked round the walls of the Kremlin at 6.30. A cool misty morning and the first smell of autumn. Rotund women cleaning the streets. They don't rise early in Moscow. Wrote letters, then went with the Gages to the Kremlin. We were taken round in company with an unpleasant-looking man in a Brigade tie, a man of incredible stupidity. ("And who is Tsar now?" was the sort of question he asked.) Later Mogs asked a guide who he was, and the guide said his name was Scurf and he was a Bedouin. The Kremlin is a good place, the Armoury Museum full of fabulous riches, priests' clothes almost knitted out of pearls, and great Wardour Street thrones of real gold, and strange weapons, and gifts, some tasteless, some exquisite, from the various kings of various countries and various ages. Very well kept. We saw the churches where the Tsars were crowned and buried and baptized, though not of course in that order. There were some soldiers drilling quite well and singing much better. We were accompanied by an amiable Red Guard with a revolver.

After that we went to the Museum of Western Art, which I saw in 1931 and under the Gauguins in which I still think you could write without offence "Come to Hawaii." They are very posterish. Then we went to a sort of registry office, where you can get married or divorced for 3 roubles (if your papers are in order; 15 roubles if they are not). The divorce : marriage ratio used to be 40 : 60, but has now gone down.[1] Both parties

[1] This sentence, from which it is impossible to discover whether marriages have increased in proportion to divorces or *vice versa*, well illustrates the diarist's ineptitude in the management of even simple statistics.

must turn up for a marriage, but only one for a divorce. The woman may keep her own name if she likes. We sat, slightly embarrassed, in a small, ugly room stinking of distemper and watched the union of a soldier with a nice face to a bovine telephonist. They were married by a plump, beady-eyed female official. In the middle of the formalities another woman suddenly rushed in with a baby in arms, but rushed out again before the relevance, if any, of this intrusion could be determined. The happy pair seemed quite indifferent to our presence, and the interpreter said that an apology would hardly be understood. Outside there was a booth selling flowers, sole vestige of the antique ballyhoo elsewhere associated with these occasions. There was, alas, no one getting divorced. We were told that applications came about equally from either sex.

Dropping Scurf, we lunched with Bullitt [then American Ambassador to Russia], where there were some pleasant French people and a very heavy American U.P. correspondent and his wife. Neither he nor Mogs could understand a word the other said. Bullitt was charming and alert. The British think him a charlatan, but you've got to be that in Russia and he seems a successful one.

I fiddled about in the afternoon, talking to Duranty and badgering Intourist, who now find that my passport is not out of order after all. Then we went to the Red Square with Boris, our interpreter for the Caucasus. He is a swarthy, seedy, shifty-looking man who claims to have been at Oxford (though his college—St. Catherine's—does not in my opinion exist); intelligent, garrulous, but lacks resource. Up to any dirty work, I should say.

In the Red Square they were holding a demonstration celebrating the 20th anniversary of the International Youth Movement, a date arbitrarily fixed to coincide with the opening of the partridge season. The streets were crowded, but rather well policed by Ogpu men in white and special constables of either sex wearing blue armbands. After being misdirected by officials the usual number of times we completed the circuit of the Kremlin and got into the Red Square from the far side. The skies were grey and it was cold. At 6.45 the big noise [Stalin] came out of the Kremlin and appeared on Lenin's mausoleum. A large band played a dreary tune, presumably the *Internationale*, and a speech was relayed through loudspeakers which made it quite incomprehensible even to Russians. But I dare say they could guess what was being said. The speaker was the head of the Komsomol called Kosarev (?). Then the march past began, the units formed up in the middle of the square, wheeling round it and saluting with bent arms.[1] Half a million people are said to have marched past, and I can well believe it. The march discipline of the troops, who were I think mostly not regulars, was pretty good considering. It varied a bit as between units. Then there were sailors, and a squad of gym instructresses, whose chest development excited the wonder of the French, and indeed my own. Probably the most popular contingent were the aviation students, and especially the parachutists. Moscow is mad about parachuting, for some unknown reason.[2] They wore dark

[1] The diarist probably means that they saluted with clenched fists.

[2] Military doctrine in England had not, in 1934, swallowed, let along digested, the conception of airborne forces. I see that in a dispatch to *The Times* (Jan. 2, 1935) I referred to parachuting as "an exercise to which young Moscow's passionate addiction seems

blue overalls and helmets and were about 10 % female. Some of them carried little aeroplanes on sticks. Then there were various sizes of Youth Pioneers, the smallest probably about 8 years old. Some of them pedalled grandly past in miniature armoured cars. They must have enjoyed it. There were quite a few sharpshooters, carrying boastfully riddled targets.

During all this we were constantly being prevented from sitting on the stone tiers which we and others rather sparsely occupied. Some soldiers behind us were not taking it very seriously. They looked tough pleasant men and I learnt a little about badges. After the military had finished the searchlights came on and all the various districts of Moscow marched past with banners, huge photographs of their rulers, "satirical floats," balloons and parachutes, and many competitive bands. It was a fine sight of the Tattoo variety, only more barbaric and spontaneous. I was due for dinner at the British Embassy and got across the river only by joining in with one of the processions which were crossing the square about 10 abreast.

Dined with William Haytor, as intelligently Wyke-hamist as ever. Charles, the Councillor, was there and a couple called Paton, late of Vladivostok. I talked too much but it was fun. Got back latish. The general atmosphere was as ill informed, as *désorienté*, and as agreeable as ever.[1]

---

a back-handed compliment to the Russian Air Force." Both in its matter and its manner, this sentence is a good example of bad reporting.

[1] A tendency to make comments of this nature on H.M. diplomatic missions in foreign capitals has long been an occupational disease among youthful travellers.

SEPTEMBER 2

Up fairly early again. Got an interpreter after various misgivings and went to see the Mongols about Urga. The Mongol Legation appeared to be in the process of being demolished and only the secretary was there, who could not see me. But I primed my interpreter suitably and scored some sort of a contact and I think there is just a chance.[1] Walked back, fiddled about, and lunched with the Gages. Mogs had been taken over a terrifying abortion clinic, George had been absorbing Town Planning and was funny about it.

The delegates to the Drama Festival are legion, and the Intourist women play high tragedy on the importunate telephone. In the afternoon we went to the Zoo with Boris, who is proving a very inaccurate man; I was excited by the sight of some enormous Siberian tigers, but the Caucasian fauna were represented chiefly by badgers. Lovely afternoon and quite fun. On the way back we stopped at the Anti-Religious Museum, which is not as funny as it ought to be and really rather ambiguous. An illiterate child would have some difficulty in deducing that it was Anti.

I have got permission for the Turksib, which is a great and unexpected thing. But it is going to be very difficult.

I wrote a rude crack in the visitors' book at the Anti-God Museum, where our cameras were confiscated, though the woman in charge could not say why; it looks as if they had not the courage of their lack of convictions. The whole place was shoddy, tumbledown, and full of irrelevancies. We came back and drank some whisky and went to the Kamerny Theatre to see *The*

[1] I was, as so often, wrong.

3   33

Optimistic Tragedy. I said in *One's Company* that the
theatre suggested the gun-turret of a battleship, and this
time it was certainly true on both side of the footlights.
The play starts on a battleship at the time of the Revolution, and is a mixture of ideology and melodrama in
which the Bolsheviks, the Interventionists, the Anarchists, and the Tsarists contend confusedly. The audience
applauded the last scene, which was pure Union Jack
Lyceum stuff, with great enthusiasm; they liked the
German soldiers being done down, they didn't give a
damn about the anarchists. An understudy in the mus-
cular Christian, Joan of Arc leading part was preferable
to Tairov's wife. We saw Tairov [the director] in the
interval. I didn't take to him. He is putting on *Antony
and Cleopatra.* But for a little buffooning the acting was
damn good, and the production excellent. I have never
seen better battle scenes. Then we came back and had
supper and I helped T. Bazley, who is here,[1] to buy an
air mail stamp. So to bed.

SEPTEMBER 3

Lovely day. A typically unsatisfactory morning in
pursuit of the Mongols, to whom I was finally obliged
to write and leave it at that. Did a little work on my
itinerary, which doesn't look like being too expensive.[2]
After lunch we drove out to bathe at the Silver Forest,
a pleasant sort of Hampstead Heath where the villas of
the lately great are transformed into rest-houses and

[1] "Who is here." The diarist at this point exhibits an attention
to detail which will strike many as superfluous.

[2] It is perhaps worth explaining that *The Times*, though it paid
at a generous rate for my dispatches, was not responsible for my
travelling expenses, and that I needed to (and in the end easily
did) make the journey pay for itself.

sanatoria for the proletariat. You reach it over a bumpy road running through a semi-devastated area of munition stores and airfields. Lot of aeroplanes about. [1] On the beach below a high bank we found a party of Titian-sized women, entirely naked and entirely ugly; also some naked men. Undeterred, we bathed (at least I did) in the swift and very shallow river, too shallow to swim, and watched a fool trying to row upstream. He remained stationary for about half an hour, but was too proud or too silly to wade and pull the boat, a very simple process which was eventually performed for him by a comrade. I was bitten by mosquitoes but felt rejuvenated. Then we went back and Duranty came in for a drink with Best, lately a correspondent in China, a nice man who was helpful about Korea. Dined with the charming Charles at the Embassy, where there was a contemporary of Richard's from Magdalen who is third secretary and a Greek ex-naval officer, ex-embezzler, full of inside stuff. Saw *The Times*, in which fears are expressed for Martin [Lindsay, then on a hazardous expedition across Greenland, now Member of Parliament for Solihull].

SEPTEMBER 4

An unsatisfactory morning, during which Boris lost his name. Got myself vaccinated, which had no effect at all. The Greek, a pure Oppenheim figure, came round and sold us a few roubles but he couldn't get many. Mogs went to the Children's Theatre and found it excellent. The drama delegates swarm everywhere. The jaded tragediennes of Intourist are hard put to it.

[1] "Lot of aeroplanes about." The diarist's powers of detailed observation are not here deployed to full advantage.

We heard one old Scots lady complaining because, although the only thing she was interested in was dentistry, she had been taken no less than four times to the same museum of Russian art. Scurf also is funny about his slumming activities.

Had an awfully nice letter from Maurice Baring about *One's Company*. In the afternoon we desultorily went to a Boyar's house and then to Lenin's tomb, where thousands still come at the appointed time but way is made for tourists. It was hot down there. Lenin,[1] who is supposed to melt periodically, seems to have shrunk since 1931. The devotees of this new religion shuffle past with a blank but politely curious expression, comprising no element of devotion.

We paid our bills, firmly rejecting apocrypha, and caught the train for Kharkov.[2] I shared a compartment with an enormous Ukrainian lady, of whom at the outset I gave to Mogs a very uncomplimentary description in English. Throughout the journey she maintained a gloomy silence and a *fatale* air. At the close of it she said, "Excuse me, please" in perfect English. It was a bad break. They treated us well on the train. We all drank too much coffee and could not sleep. The fat woman, in a violet light, lay below me like an enormous snowdrift.

SEPTEMBER 5

Reached Kharkov at noon on a cloudless windy day. It is a bright clean progressive-looking place, very impressive. They did us well at the hotel, providing for

---

[1] He is, of course, embalmed.
[2] On our way south to the Caucasus.

breakfast caviar and other of our national dishes. Our interpreter was charming. A delegation of 60 French schoolteachers was also visiting the town, and a substantial number of Czekoslovakians have arrived since. None can say why.

After lunch we drove round the town, then George had one of his planning interviews with the big shots, and Mogs and I went miles away and bathed with some difficulty in a stormy river which did us a lot of good and strengthened the impression of eccentricity which I hope to create. Then we were taken over the Palace of Culture, which is a very well-architected railway workers' club with a theatre and a broadcasting station and all. Unfortunately the workers were not there. There is always something missing in Russia. After dinner we went to a fantastic function, a reception to the French teachers. On a dais draped with banners, three dentists (I am pretty sure) attacked with fury three xylophones. A woman sang songs in all the dialects of Russia. There was a Spanish dance, a Dutch dance, and more songs by the daughter of a poet. The delegates awaited the arrival of something to eat with unconcealed impatience. I wrote letters.

SEPTEMBER 6

At 10 o'clock we set out for a *kolhoz* [collective farm]. It was a biggish village lying in flat but slightly rolling country. The white Ukrainian houses with thatched roofs and tiny unopenable windows looked very pleasant in the sunshine. We were soon taken in charge by the local party secretary, a tough, insular young man, the power in that place. We tasted their honey and prodded their pigs and Mogs drove one of their buggies. The farm produces mostly vegetables. 20% of its produce is sold at a nominal price to the Government, the rest in the open market. Fertiliser supplied by the Government had had a good effect. There was a small land tax. The most interesting thing was the degree of kulakism allowed now. Everyone had his own garden or allotment and was allowed to keep pigs or cows, though no one as it happened had more than two or three of either; potatoes were 3 kopeks per kg. to the Government, 50 in the open market; 70% of the workers were women. We saw rather polite children eating bortsch in the *crêche*, and the cooperative store, which sold almost nothing except vodka, matches, and very shoddy clothes. Almost all the houses had the radio. In the one we went into the walls were prettily painted; Kaganovitch [then, and up to the time of going to press, a member of the Politburo] shared the wall with an ikon. Everything reasonably clean. We lunched in their eating-place off bortsch, black bread, potatoes, tomatoes, and melons.

When we got back George and I went over some flats with an architect, who said that the work done to his designs was about 30% unsatisfactory. Architects have a pretty free hand here. The flats all seemed to me good: light and spacious and cheap. In the first there was a man, a pre-war Bolshevik, who had done 13 years' solitary confinement but conspicuously possessed a sense of humour. He had his shackles hanging up in his bedroom. Then there was one belonging to an architect with some rather amusing pictures done by the tenant; it was refreshing to find evidence of some sort of taste somewhere. He had *Robinson Crusoe* on his bookshelf. I heard some children exclaiming at it in a shop yesterday; it is in brisk demand here. Then there was another poorer flat, but still quite adequate.

After that we went to the races, which turned out to be trotting races. They were fairly well attended and there was some primitive system of betting. But not much enthusiasm. The jockeys were fantastic mid-Victorian figures, and had great difficulty in preventing the scratch horses from galloping, which they are allowed to do for only four strides. The jockeys are professionals, but the horses amateurs from the farms, which race against each other.

We were to have flown to Rostov tomorrow, but the wind is considered too high. So we must catch a train at 3 a.m.

Later. It didn't of course turn up till 4, and proved to be without the advertised dining car. We boarded it stupid with fatigue, after wandering about the streets for a long time. They were empty save for a certain number of indefinite night-watchmen sitting on chairs in front of doors. There was also an old man who suddenly stooped, picked up a fragment of newspaper from the gutter, and put it on a window sill. I thought he was going to roll a cigarette, but he produced instead a little bird from his pocket and wrapped it up in the paper. It had hit the telegraph wires and cut its head. He was very sorry for it, but I don't know what good the newspaper was. The head waiter at the hotel was a romantic figure, an effective ex-prospector, ex-East Side waiter, ex-stage dancer in U.S.A. The depression had driven him back to Russia.

Got to sleep about 5 in the morning.

SECOND STAGE

TO THE CAUCASUS

TO THE CAUCASUS

SEPTEMBER 6

Woke at noon. Boris was snoring with precision. A long day running inordinately slowly (on account of the bad permanent way) through flat and limitless country. Pretty hot. Ate buns and bad fruit and read Renier's *Oscar Wilde*. He is a good writer, engagingly sardonic. We reached Rostov about 7, half an hour late, after skirting for some time the Sea of Azov. All the peasants at the stations looked well and had lots of tomatoes, melons, eggs, etc., to sell. Installed in a rather ambitious hotel: splendid baths but no hot water. That sort of thing, but very good on the whole. The main street looks cheerful and vaguely Brazilian. People in white clothes shuffling up and down and talking incessantly. Dined and wrote some letters and found that we have to stay here a day longer than we meant to.

SEPTEMBER 7

Started at 10 for a big agricultural implement factory. Here work appeared to be proceeding rather spasmodically, under conditions which are very enlightened on paper. The things that interested me most were that 43% of the workers are women; that each shock brigade, controlled by its own brigadier, pillories bad workers by name with bad caricatures on its notice-board—

another echo of the Moscow Park stuff; that every worker's rest period of an hour is preceded by 5 minutes compulsory P.T.; that Shock Workers have a silly little banner on their bit of machinery. Chiefly, in fact, the Montessorian atmosphere. In the club library questions and answers were posted on the notice-board. One was, "Where can I study man's struggle for existence?" The answer was "Fill up a form and in the meantime read these books." Another was "Why no books by Jules Verne, Mayne Reid, and Fenimore Cooper?" The answer was that Verne was all to the good, but Cooper and Reid misrepresented American exploitation of the indigenes and were chauvinistic and imperialistic. We saw also workers' flats and a closed shop, where white bread was selling for 60 kopeks instead of 10 roubles and meat for 3 roubles instead of 9. Had the usual dilatory lunch, then George went to interview a judge while Mogs and I sat in a public garden and read and talked.

Then we all went on the Don in a motor boat with the director of Intourist, an insufferable young American-educated candidate for the Communist party. This is holding a purge tomorrow, and he is therefore aggressively orthodox. He also seems unhappy here. We bathed in shallow black mud, very nice though I spiked my foot on a fish bone and lost a cuff link. The sky was lovely coming back. I had a glass of sour wine with Boris, who told me he got 60 roubles an hour for coaching actors who had to play the part of foreigners—e.g. Cooper in *Tempo*. There is a lot of money to be made in the theatre, and it seems to hold a pretty high position in cultural life.

After dinner we went to a cinema, probably the worst

I have ever seen. It began with a black blurred picture of salvage work in the Black Sea, devoid of interest or comprehensibility. Then there was a fearful comedy, sooty and prehistoric. We walked out.

SEPTEMBER 9 (one day seems to have been left out)

Started at 10 for the state farm at Zernograd. Held up for half an hour at the very inadequate bridge over the Don, while horse-drawn traffic zigzagged up the hill behind us, mostly on all fours. Once away, however, the Lincoln, extremely well driven, maintained a dizzy speed along a dirt road which wandered rather inconsequently over the steppe. A strong wind was against us and it was impossible to keep your eyes open. If you did, they were immediately filled with the dust, which was terrific. After two hours' drive through flat country, melancholy rather than cheerless, we arrived, black with dust. We had passed little save two foundered lorries and a surprising variety of hawks. We lunched with an unimpressive guide in the communal restaurant where they gave us quite good meat and where we met a fantastic American farmer, a shrivelled fatalistic figure who had lost his all and was engaged here at 300 roubles a month as a grain expert. There followed the usual shuffling procession round half-baked institutions, the usual tirade of statistics. They had 9,000 people on the farm, though only 1,500 agricultural labourers. They had no police and no militia, but crime (they said) was unknown. The yield per hectare was going up. They sowed with aeroplanes when the ground was too soft for ordinary sowing. Nobody seemed to be doing any work anywhere, but there was always an excuse.

45

On the way back we called at a dairy farm (state), assimilating more statistics and milk. Russia is like Ruth Draper's garden.

SEPTEMBER 10

While the others submitted to the inevitable milk factory I set out with Boris on the loose. After several false starts we finished up in a People's District Court, the best show Russia has provided thus far. It was sitting in a hot room in a dim house in a dim street. We inadvertently took our places with the accused, and were moved. There were perhaps 40 people present, say 10 prisoners, 6 Ogpu guards with fixed bayonets and a lackadaisical manner, and various unplaceable spectators, often with babies. "Speak English?" said one of the prisoners, a cheerful man. Presently the judge came in and the court unexpectedly stood up. He was a reliable-looking man with a fine face, like a younger Gerald du Maurier. He sat at a red-covered table, under the inevitable picture of Lenin. He was flanked by the two co-judges, who are elected by the workers and who consisted of a good-looking, rather French woman with spaniel eyes, about 30—the familiar Y.W.C.A. type of the Russian films—and an older woman, probably not as old as she looked. She was splendid. Her face was full of wrinkles and wisdom, very shrewd and of necessity a little disillusioned. She sat hunched like a crone, very alert. Under a red scarf her blue eyes moved in her face like lizards in a wall. (But she was very matter-of-course about it all—not putting herself out at all.) The judges looked a good gang.

The first case heard had nothing to do with this

46

court, which was suppo
offenders. It was a woman c
from the railway for which s
squat Jewish representative of th
front of the Bench while the judge
pointing out that she could still appea
if she wished.

Then the judge called a name, and a dar
bearded man came forward. He was accused
4 passports and 4 sheets of paper with the se
unit for which he worked (it was a hydrogra
geological station or something). He said he was a
smith. He gave his father's name and his own a
wrong, and was unable to produce all the papers he
should have. He admitted the theft with (like a child)
one minor reservation, and pleaded that he had stolen
the passes in order to enable his sister, who had been
disenfranchised for belonging to the kulak class, to go
on living in their village. The sealed paper he meant to
use to get food for his family.

He was sent miserably back to his seat to await
sentence, which is delivered at the end of the day. In
the middle of an impassioned speech by the next de-
fendant he suddenly found in his pocket one of the
papers which they wanted, and produced it with a glad
cry. Nobody took much notice.

The next prisoner was a girl of 19, in a mauve blouse
and a dirty tartan skirt. She had a pert, rather brutish
face, lounged against a bench, gave several false names,
denied having had her fingerprints taken, and said,
"Why? Can't you see me?" when told to speak up and
come closer. She had been caught red-handed stealing
a bale of cloth from a shop. She pleaded economic

47

t's funny
l.

illiterate
d head.
t could
He had
twice,
used of
r in a
pped
they
the
ture
im,
vas
with whom he
black bread.

sed to deal with hardened
laiming wages for overtime
e worked. She and the
e railway stood up in
dismissed her case,
l to a higher court
k, shambling,
of stealing
al of the
hical-
ock-

...yone was sweating. One of the Ogpu men tried to open a window but gave it up.)

The next case was a boy in a blue zephyr, 22 and earning 175 a month in a store. He said he held an administrative position there, but created a bad impression, poor dear, by being unable to define what he meant by administrative. He had no police record, but claimed to belong to the Metalworkers Trade Union, which did him no good, because it had apparently lately been dissolved into something else. He looked a nice chap. He was accused of stealing a pair of top boots from the market. His defence was that he had merely picked up an old pair of shoes with wooden soles which were lying in the gutter.

At this point Boris and I left, but were sent for by the judge, who received us in a back room. He was very nice. He looked smaller than he had in court, and once more I was reminded of an actor. He explained that this court was for hardened offenders, and that no witnesses were called because the defendants had always been caught virtually red-handed. I asked him what sort of a sentence the man whose sister was a kulak would get, but he couldn't say, because he and the co-judges hadn't discussed it all. Then I said, was I right in guessing that the first offender in the blue zephyr would get a fairly light sentence? The judge pointed out that his lying about the boots made his offence much more serious; but it seemed to me that it was only his word against the policeman's, and therefore rough luck. The judge also talked a certain amount of rot about knowing the formation of a criminal's skull when they saw it. General impression: they would have been much better judges if they had known nothing about Soviet ideology and the Progress cranks. The police work involved in the way of dossiers and fingerprints seemed to be good. I took their photograph, though of course they didn't look half so good as they had in court. But they were tickled to death, and very anxious to know when they could expect a copy.

In the afternoon we all went back to the Court, to find that it had risen but that there was a more or less civil action going on in another room. Eight assorted people, with little in common save their bewilderment, were accused of indenting for more freight cars than were needed and thus balling up the Five Year Plan. Shrewd monkey-faced judge, flanked by a sour spinster and a peasant woman. Two white-shirted bullet-headed lawyers at desks below the rails. All smoked intermittently.

First hour and a half devoted to identification. During this process the accused were questioned closely about their parents ("social background"), education, and especially war record. Almost everyone in Rostov has been in the White Army at one time or another. These were all concerned to prove that they had been impressed into it. One *simpatico* young man got into deep waters through being unable to remember such details of that haphazard campaigning in his early youth as the number of his Division, the name of his C.O., etc.

During all this time the charge was not mentioned at all. The atmosphere was friendly as well as informal, though a sense of injustice seemed to hover over the accused, as well it probably might. There were no guards, and the accused came and went as they pleased. The whole thing was clearly none of their fault. I was reminded once more of the rabbits story.[1]

In the evening we were to have seen the bank manager purged, but the presiding genius was said to be ill, so we couldn't. We dined off sweet champagne, bought cheap for roubles by Boris. Caught the train,

[1] As far as I can remember, this story went something like this: A new law was passed forbidding camels to emigrate from the U.S.S.R. At about the same time the rabbits, who were sick to death of life in Russia, decided to go and live abroad. When they reached the frontier the Frontier Guards stopped them and asked them what they were doing.

"We're emigrating," the rabbits answered.

"You can't do that," said the Frontier Guards.

"Why not?" asked the rabbits.

"There is a new law," said the Frontier Guards, "which expressly forbids camels to emigrate."

"But we're not camels!" cried the rabbits.

"You try telling that to the Ogpu," said the Frontier Guards, and put them all under arrest.

which was 40 minutes late. They were of course uncertain up to the last moment whether there were
sleepers for us, and had brought rolls of bedding in case.
Boris was in fantastic argumentative form, owing, I
later discovered, to a tumbler of vodka.

SEPTEMBER 11

At 7 p.m. I find that my food so far today has been,
in the following order, 1 omelette, 1 cup of coffee, 4
cups of tea, 2 glasses of champagne, and 1 chocolate
biscuit. The train turned out not to go to Ordjhonikidze,
so we detrained, late as usual, at a place called Breslan,
or something, where I believe there is a syrup unit.
Drove for an hour through heavy rain towards mist-
hidden mountains over black liquescent roads. Occasionally a child threw a stick at us. When the car skidded
worse than usual the driver, a good man, said "F-fox-
t-trot" and grinned. We passed dank carts, grey river in
spate, men in wide white felt hats beaten floppy by the
rain. Ordjhonikidze looked a dim place. A barefoot
squad of prisoners was being marched aimlessly through
the torrential streets, which even under the shadow of
the Caucasus were not without their tram. In the clean,
unattractive hotel we debated our route with the usual
charming collection of ignorami, who included one
sensible Hungarian. A car was sent up to Kasbek for
the local expert, but he never appeared.

Spotted and went to *Sailors of the King*, a film based
on the Invergordon mutiny. Very funny. Locale
wavered inconsequently between tropical and home
waters. Heroine's employer forced her to marry him
during absence of the Sailor Clarence, her true love.
Heroine's housing conditions pointedly shown to be

unsatisfactory. Policemen wearing firemen's helmets. Someone wrote "Colonies, look out for your purses" on a revolving gun-turret. Visitant rajah suitably perturbed. "Miss Molly's" souvenirs were preponderantly Jap, which was meant to be significant, I think. When the sailors mutinied the officers said, "Very well, we will haul up the anchor ourselves." "If you do," said the sailors, "we will let down the other anchor." In the end the sailors got their cuts restored and Lt. Watson, who had slapped one of them on the wrist, was sent ashore. But they all fell in obediently at the end of the film, which thus seemed to me ineffective even as propaganda. Incidentally the officers searched the men's kit while the latter were taking part in what appeared to be a rock-climbing competition in full kit. Almost throughout the film two orchestras, one in the theatre, one in the foyer, were in full blast. This worried everyone except me.[1]

Curious ideas, incidentally, seem to prevail about our police. I read a speech in which they were described as "laying aside their rubber truncheons" in some crisis.

Did some repacking and then drank wine in the garden with Boris and an amiable, cropped, corpulescent painter who had served with him in Turkestan and had studied painting in Paris under Derain. He was a naïve, enthusiastic man, earning some 50,000 roubles a year, mostly from railway companies and so on. Showed me some of his pictures, which were lousy. He was formerly a joiner. Via patronised art and Shakespeare, I got on to an argument with Boris who said that England was a very backward country. As proof he instanced an egg and spoon race round a park at

[1] The diarist is preternaturally unmusical.

Oxford, in which he had been compelled to take part in 1913. Also the "petrol lamps in the students' cottages," and the incessant psalm-singing on Sundays in all respectable English homes. He has a weak head.

SEPTEMBER 12

Up at 6. Roared up the Georgian Military Highway towards the clouds. This road had been repeatedly described as being "as smooth as a mirror" but was not. Splendid bit of (Tsarist) engineering, which wound up gorges with a steep drop on the off side. Driver reckless but very good. Damn cold. Terrific scenery. Stopped and drank brandy at Kasbek. The mountain of that name (16,545 feet high)[1] was hidden. Later went over the Cross Pass, which is 7,000 feet high. Road is closed by snow (against which there are tunnels and walls) from November to May. Dropped tortuously down to Passanour, a little village where we had some food and picked up two guides and some three-legged horses.[2] After the usual ineffectual English struggle to better the lot of such of the latter as were obviously on the point of collapse, we set off, mostly on foot, up a valley towards the Hevsur territory.

After a long wait half-way while another horse was scrounged out of some eyrie in the crags, we went on. It began to rain like stink. At 5.30, soaked through, we reached some sort of a village and quartered ourselves in a two-storey building which contained a wool store, a shop, the police station, and some nondescript gendarmerie. Here we ate our cold food and boiled some Oxo, the water for which I procured by the simple ex-

[1] It is certainly higher than this.
[2] See photograph opposite p. 56.

pedient of holding the saucepan under the gout of rain-water from the eaves. My thick sweater had been lost, but one of the men rode back and found it. It was very cold, but my Bagdad sheepskin coat was a godsend and much admired by the natives. I slept in it and my clothes dried on me. We got bags of wool for beds, very comfortable. But Mogs was kept awake by insects, and I for some reason got very little sleep, reading Malraux until a late hour. There was a mysterious deposit of bantams' eggs in our room, and a fair showing of rats. White Knight Gage had a lot of useful stuff in his valise. It was great fun, in the lamp-light exactly like a melo-drama about the Canadian Mounted Police.

SEPTEMBER 13

Still pouring when we woke at 5.30. Got off before 7, forcing the men to abandon a very badly lamed horse which collapsed in the mud when mounted. The cossack saddles are hell to ride with the short leathers which prevail. We made off up the very rocky bed of a river, which we had to wade (only Mogs was riding) re-peatedly. It was fine wild country[1]. Boris, swathed in pyjamas and other oddments, perched miserably and maladroitly on a horse. For some reason his face seemed to go quite black. We took with us only one guide, an effective but cruel boy who was half Hevsur. After about 3 hours we did a steep short climb and reached the Hevsur village.

The tribe is said to number 10,000. Most of them live further over the mountains, are alleged to be hostile, and do not recognise the Soviets. Ours were dour but charming. They are supposed to be descended from

[1] See photograph between pp. 56–57.

Crusaders under Godfrey of Boulogne, and this was borne out by the sort of mailed leather jerkins which they wore, the crosses on their shoulders, and the fact that they used some word sounding like "English" for *Angleeski*. They were unsmiling, fine-looking men in fur hats. They had some good swords and knives, but none very old. The best house had two storeys with a room for the cattle in the winter. They are said to be great hunters. They were the first people I have seen in Russia to inspire respect. They would give us no food— in fact we gave them a lot—because they won't let any-one else eat out of their pots. There was some good carving on a chest, and a swinging cylinder in which they made butter. They gave us some home-made spirit which was weak and tasted like furniture polish. They had a fine situation, looking down into the twisted valley and up into the snows. There was also a Chechen man there, by comparison a grinning oaf with less breed-ing in his face. On one of the dresses they showed us there was a coin fastened on to the breast. It was a late Victorian sixpenny bit. I augmented their collection with a George V.

We had a long way to go, so started down about noon. Ate some food in the sun (which had now come out) by a Georgian farm, closely watched by the Peasant Clarence, a very inscrutable boy who had qualms about eating cheese for fear that it was made of pig. As we were starting off I discovered that my haversack had dropped off a led horse. It contained my passport, my letter of indication, my Kodak, razor, torch, pyjamas, comb, a book, some tobacco, and films, and was on account of the first item a serious loss. Without much hope I let the others go on and rode back with the

Hevsur boy, a dreary ride on a lifeless horse. He went up to the village and came back to say that someone had been seen departing into the mountains with some object found on the trail, and that the Hevsurs would get it back and send it on. It sounds moderately hopeful, though I have since found that my mackintosh was also lost, so the object may quite well have been that. It is bad luck, but I expect I can manage without the passport.[1]

It was now 2 o'clock. We clattered endlessly down the river bed. I alternately rode and towed my horse. At the place where we had slept I heard that the others had left an hour ago, so put on steam and practically carried my horse into Passanour only half an hour behind them. It was awfully like coming back from stalking. It was a hard day, over 30 miles, but I felt grand. George was too stiff to move, but all right the next day.

It was now dusk. We wrapped up in everything we had, left Boris to badger the Ogpu about my haversack, and drove 90 cold kilometres down to Tiflis talking about religion while Mogs's small head in a flying helmet toppled about in a drugged way in the front seat. The warm and hospitable hotel we invaded in a curious procession—me in my savage furs, Mogs looking like an eccentric step-dancer in George's trousers, and George in his stockinged feet carrying his shoes.

Glad to get my boots off.

SEPTEMBER 14

Planning and seeing the sights. Tiflis is attractive, the old Perso-Armenian-Georgian quarter dotted with the stubby silver spires of churches. An old Persian fortress

[1] A foolish assertion.

commands the town. A yellow river, the Koura, runs through it, while the population fishes sporadically from its balconies. The bazaar has just been destroyed, native costume is no longer the vogue, and only cheap, shoddy, scanty Russian goods fill the shops in the old quarter. The whole place in short is going through the usual vulgarisation and standardisation. Our best moment was in the wine cellars of Samtrest [the State Wine Trust], where George and I were required to drink five different sorts of wine, finishing up with champagne, out of the same glass and on an empty stomach. I was unaffected, but Boris expanded horribly, and our interpreter, the worst-dressed woman I have ever seen, became both loud and redundant in her utterances. It was very funny indeed. A little old goat-like man, with experience of viticulture in France, was there. He had a permanently bibulous face, but toasted us very nicely. The vice-director of Samtrest gave us a bottle of wine for Mogs, and George wrote politely in the visitors' book. The Georgians are human.

I missed lunch and talked to the archaeologist Brown, a red-haired, very intelligent Old Etonian attached to the (Burroughs and) Wellcome Museum, who has been doing his stuff out here. He sees Stalin's régime as doomed, and the power going to the Red Army, who he claims have already been approached by the Ogpu begging for quarter when the time comes.

We drove out in sun and fierce wind to Mskhet, Stalin's birthplace and the ancient capital of Georgia. There was a lovely monastery on a hill, and a goodish 5th-century church which we inspected with a noble monk. Also a nunnery (?), less good. The road was good, but the straight stretches were more or less invalidated by the chronic inability of anyone to get out of the way in time.

We discussed plans with our hunter and the intelligent manager of the hotel, then dined, while Brown told strange stories of his aunt and Mitchell Hedges, then went to a most irrelevant ceremony. This was a celebration of some centenary of the Persian poet Firdaussi. It took place in the Railway Workers' Park. A stand under an awning was crowded with people. Far away at the other end, under a cataract of red banners, the local dignitaries sat on a dais. A professor was making an impassioned and gesticulatory speech into a loud-speaker. This, however, was a poor instrument, only audible when it emitted a prolonged shriek, and every-one at the back was talking at the tops of their voices. Presently chairs were brought for us and we were forced up the aisle and plunked down in the front row, of which from time to time cameramen with fantastic machines took photographs with the aid of arc lamps which sizzled loudly. At this range, the Professor, funny even at a distance, was absolutely irresistible. It was better still when he sat down, a military band played a few chords, and a little Persian poet, looking like a weedier Vincent Massey, got up to make his speech. "Ladies and gentlemen" he said (I suppose) in a voice vibrant with emotion; and all the lights went out. I was almost sick with laughter. In time they went on again. He finished his speech and it was translated. Then I went home, leaving George and Mogs to listen to the Georgian and Persian music, which they found almost as funny. I did a creditable bit of path-finding back to the hotel, passing on the way two men of a very cheerful kind who were settling down for the night in a municipal dustbin.

Visited the State University, a large building whose corridors were thronged with aimless, noisy students of all ages in spite of the fact that it was not term time. As in all Russian buildings, redecoration was going on apace. Interviewed the director, a highly orthodox man who talked nonsense when cornered, e.g. about old intellectuals applying for a professorship: 80% of their teachers are old intellectuals; 65% of the students are on a scholarship basis. All must study philosophy and political economy; otherwise they specialise. The library, a series of untidy cellars where the books, if arranged at all, were arranged according to size, had a lot of old-fashioned English books—Braddon, Louisa M. Alcott, etc. In the catalogue *Elizabeth and her German Garden* was attributed to Elinor Glyn. Here we established contact, with all due camouflage, with a White professor, who ventilated his ill-defined sympathies in incomprehensible French. Then George and Mogs went to the Botanical Gardens, where there were no flowers at all, while I called at the Rustavely Theatre and interviewed the local Reinhardt, Achmetely.

He was a fine histrionic-looking man of the Basil Sydney type, who received me at the head of the inevitable red-covered table. He talked a lot about how he was going to make the theatre true to Georgia; also about his revival of old national sports, like football with 5,000 a side, horse-racing with a boy on your shoulders, and a kind of mounted game of hunt-the-slipper with a sheep as the slipper. Described his super-subtle methods of interpretation. Said that the bazaar had been pulled down by some local municipal authority. Re his forthcoming production of *Julius Caesar* said that what worried him was the fact that both Caesar and Brutus, with the ideas they stood for, fell. There must be some third factor to account for this. Rome was the important thing. Very orthodox about the stage as a vehicle for ideology. Shakespeare would have had a good laugh. Finished up rather paradoxically by saying that Europe was stifling the theatre by making it a theatre of thought and philosophy; he wanted to make it a free, spontaneous form of expression. This was slightly ridiculous after all his pedantry.

Nothing much else happened today. We went to buy a razor and some socks in Torgsin [a State-run shop for foreigners]. There were no socks worth buying and the razor is hopeless. The transaction took fifty minutes, and even then they couldn't give us the right change.

In Torgsin there were a lot of men selling cheques. One of these, an American-speaking Turk, explained the racket. They get the cheques in return for gold or valuta [foreign currency], then sell them to the customers for roubles, which are not accepted in Torgsin. It was all being done quite openly. He sometimes made 40 or 50 roubles profit in a day. He offered me 220 for a £. Farce rages in this country.[1]

We then had a hot sulphur bath in some sort of catacombs and were massaged by a demoniac-looking man. When I came out I asked for a comb at the desk and an old lady took one out of her hair and offered it to me. After a huge dinner we caught the train for Telav in a wholly unnecessary rush. I slept in my boots in a soft compartment with three men who grossly underrated the value of ventilation. Much talk of the fine hunting at Telav. The train moved through the night at a foot's pace.

[1] The official rate was six or seven roubles to the £.

SEPTEMBER 16

Reached Telav, where I shaved on the sunny platform until a car arrived. It was the longest car I have
seen, driven by a man who looked like a Tasmanian
devil. We bounded over the dusty road to a pleasant
little town with a ruined fortress in the middle. A house,
it was said, was being prepared for us by the local
Soviet. In the meantime we put our luggage in a hotel,
ordered breakfast in one restuarant, and ate it in
another. Sour milk, cocoa, mutton, and wine. General
impression strongly in favour of the Georgians. Nobody
knew where our house was, so we waited about on a
balcony in the sun.

Then suddenly people appeared, fairly heavily armed,
who said they could not imagine why we had been sent
to Telav. It was all a mistake. We must go and live in
a palace at Tsinondali, where the accommodation and
the shooting were much better. We piled once more into the car, which reminds me a good deal of La Tarasque, and drove about 8 km. Crossed the bed of a dried-
up river, above which cypress-like trees crowned a queer
cliff and concealed the palace. Then up a drive through
vineyards, and so to the palace. It had belonged to the
Chavchavadzes and was a squat, creeper-covered building with deep tropical verandahs, standing in a sort of
garden-park with many different kinds of trees. We
were installed in the so-called museum apartments. In
George and Mogs's room there are 5 beds, 21 Empire
chairs in olive-green silk, 5 tables, 3 sofas, and a large
number of curious spittoons fitted with a pedal. Mine is
less magnificent, being a passage room between one
occupied by a Russian writer and his wife and the bathroom, which they tell me smells. There are 3 beds, and

although I go to bed alone there is always some absolutely unexplained man sleeping in one of the other beds when I wake up.

When we had settled into these fantastic quarters we went out shooting. A painful drive in the car, which in addition to us contained seven armed men and a dog called Rosa. Then a long aimless walk, never in line, through a wilderness of weeds, maize-fields, and scrub. Total bag: 2 quail and 2 very small doves. I was shooting with an old English 16-bore, of which the second barrel seldom fired. We should have had 2 or 3 pheasants. The best moment was when Constantin, our bodyguard, fired at a hen pheasant with his Mauser. The range was about 300 yds. and the bird was flying strongly. It is typical of this amusing expedition that the old man whom we interviewed in Tiflis, the alleged king of all this sporting district, has never reappeared. Constantin, his son, says he has hurt his arm in Tiflis. But nobody refers to him who was to have been the leader and organiser of the whole show.

We got back after dark, having eaten nothing since breakfast. The palace is now the HQ of a state vineyard, and we had a delicious dinner with the vicedirector, a noncommittal, tough, Lenin-like man who has worked here for thirty-four years. Lashings of white wine and brandy, many toasts, and big talk about shooting plans. The old servant-woman is a good figure who has taken to me because (I think) I know a Chavchavadze in London. Her husband was the old Prince's valet, and she has been here for 35 years. Remembers Alexander III coming to stay and bringing his son. Reels off pedigrees with enthusiasm in bad Russian. Plump and witch-like and benign.

SEPTEMBER 17

We were up at 5, but Boris and the men had had a blind and we didn't start till much later. By this time the pheasants were all back in thick cover and poor sport was shown. But it was great fun and lovely weather.

We drove down into the valley in sort of jaunting cars, accompanied by 4 nondescript dogs with high reputations. The clouds on the peaks opposite seem to be permanent, but the country looked very beautiful in the sunlight. We were accompanied by nine men—Sandino, so-called from his resemblance to the Nicaraguan brigand of that name, a cheerful, childish, silly man, worthless as a shot, 3 years a prisoner of war in Germany; the Japanese Admiral, a squat, rather irrelevant figure; Constantin, tall and hawk-like but suffering from a fearful hangover[1]; Tigran, also tall but rather a bumpkin, apparently a soldier, said to be responsible for our personal safety, wears a revolver and pink suspenders; a rather operative blackish boy in command of the dogs; two other blackish men, with no distinguishing characteristics; Boris, lame and miserable, trailing along in a horrible green overcoat, eating blackberries; the local expert, president of the hunting society, very nice but quite futile, wearing a white jacket. At one time and another there seemed to be others, but those were the main *dramatis personae*.

After wandering along and putting up one or two pheasants in dense cover, the expedition got completely lost in a thicket. The dogs had disappeared, allegedly in pursuit of a wolf, and morale was low. But several splendid things had happened. Sandino, for instance,

[1] See photograph between pp. 56–57.

had blown his gun like a horn in order to attract Rosa.[1]
The left barrel, being choked, gave out a higher and
more pleasing note than the other.

We sagged on, in no sort of formation and on no sort
of plan, seeing little and getting nothing, until we came
to the river (Alazan) where the droshkies were waiting
for us. Here we ate mutton and eggs and chicken and
cheese and drank a good deal of wine. After lunch fairly
heavy firing broke out. Mogs, though claiming to be
blind, broke a bottle at the first attempt. I put a target
on a tree and tried out the Mauser, which is a good
weapon and with which Constantin proved himself a
very good shot. People were standing about and shooting quite vaguely in every direction. Mogs tried a min-
now in the river without success, but the men admired
the tackle a lot and kept on bringing crickets and flies
for bait.

In the afternoon we went vaguely on, and in the end
Mogs shot two pheasants rather unexpectedly and I got
a quail and a hare, whose throat Sandino cut. The expedition got lost several times, and was also frequently
attacked by savage sheepdogs. Sandino had two shots
at fish in the river, one with a gun and one with a rifle.
Neither was successful. It was very hot. We finally made,
as they thought, for the droshkies, but these turned out
not to be where they were supposed to be, and we had
a longish walk. Mogs commandeered a horse from a
man who was carrying a bundle of small trees and he
gave it up without a murmur. Among the rank and file
of the expedition some rather wanton small-bird shooting broke out. A puppy turned up from somewhere. A
small snake was caught and put in a bottle. A large

[1] See photograph between pp. 56–57.

number of water melons were commandeered from a field and eaten. March discipline was poor.

On the way back Georgi, one of the dim blackish men, suddenly invited the whole lot of us into his house for a drink. We climbed up on to the balcony and found a very clean room with good carpets hanging on the walls and two polite children. His wife was very nice and taught in a school. A super-jeroboam of red wine was produced, also bread, cheese, sweets made from nuts and grapes, fruit, and tea. Many toasts, Sandino being at the top of his form. We ate and drank them out of house and home, which seems to be the custom in Georgia, got back two hours late for dinner (I walked the last two miles beside the horses, thus getting into a state where I could appreciate a cold bath), and ate another huge meal with the vice-director, in the course of it deciding to leave for Lagodekhi next day.

I feel grand and have gone black.

SEPTEMBER 18–30 (the rest of the alleged hunting trip)

Next day we had a date with the boys to eat the game we had shot, the hare to be specially cooked in vinegar. So decided to leave at 3. Went over the wine cellars in the morning, with a mercifully mild drinking bout and an abacus race. Lunch was a vast meal, with Sandino in terrific form as *tamada*.[1] They spotted George as a military man, me as the reverse. Much wine drunk to my unborn children. Meanwhile a forester had turned up with the news of a bear, but after deciding to spend the night in pursuit of it we scrapped the whole thing as a canard. At 3 no signs of the car. At 5 the Tarasque

[1] A sort of master of ceremonies at Georgian social functions.

appeared with a truculent driver, no lights, and no petrol. Terrific argument. By 6 we had driven ten miles in the wrong direction and found ourselves after several breakdowns back in Telav. A typical scene ensued. Lorries and an aeroplane were all promised in turn, crowds collected, and at last when all seemed lost an antediluvian charabanc was found which would take us as far as Kvareli. They took two hours to get it ready and change the wheel, but finally we started down the appalling road with one blinking light and the usual complement of unexplained passengers. Drive rendered eventful by many river beds and several hares which drew a murderous or rather suicidal fire from guns and rifles. Tigran almost blew Mogs's head off. Passed an incredibly romantic monastery perched on a rock and reached Kvareli about 11.

Here we lodged in a dilapidated and inconvenient house, feeding in a restaurant half a mile of black mud away, where the food was sometimes very good and sometimes non-existent and where we ate quantities of *matsoni*, a sour milk which is very good with sugar. On the 19th, after the usual 3 or 4 hours' delay, we had a pheasant shoot, even less effective than the former ones, and very hard work among the hot maize fields. We shot a few quail and saw little else, but in the evening when we had knocked off, the men suddenly found a spot and got 10 pheasants. Had an awfully good dinner with red wine and slept in our bags on the blood-specked beds.

An early start was promised for the 20th, but we got off about 5 hours late after the usual fetching of horses and dogs and getting permission from the local Soviet. Under a heavy rain we drove a short distance in unnecessary buggies, then climbed, a considerable force, into the wooded hills. The men wore old military overcoats, looked like Third Murderers, and shambled steaming through the mist like bears. All were heavily armed. The two drives came to nothing at all, though I saw a squirrel and one of the beaters shot a young gazelle like a roe. We had a sharp slide down and an unaccountably bad dinner. The usual burst of target practice in the middle of the shoot.

On the 21st, later than ever, we marched out along the foothills in blazing sunshine, had one promising but blank drive where deer were seen, and camped idyllically quite low down in the woods. It really was lovely. We tore up chunks of meat and swigged wine in front of an enormous fire. The men got rather drunk on some kind of vodka and did wild Georgian dances to their knives, singing like fiends and clapping their hands. The chief of them is Archie, whose real name is Achilles, a lined, goatlike figure much burdened with firearms. Our bodyguard, Cote or Constantin, is good, but the best of them is Maxim, an ex-major in the Tsarist army, a man of courage, humour, and charm. They are all good on the hill, though foolish.

On the 22nd we had a terrific day, climbing and sliding down, but all to no purpose, except that I saw a badger in the first drive, Maxim shot a small wild-cat with a ringed tail, and Cote, who had been left in camp, got some kind of a roe of which we made *shashlik*. All the drives went wrong, the last, which meant the hardest climb for the guns, worst of all, the beaters and dogs just disappearing. Archie, who plays the old aristocrat, dismissed them as worthless and "*Sovietski*." Reunited at last, we left them altercating in the greenwood and

67

staggered home in the hot sun, passing a man who can only be described as a pig-charmer. He sat by the bank of a stream and from time to time uttered a curious, low, despondent cry; the fairy-like pigs came galloping.

We found that Boris had got a car from Tiflis but that the spring was broken. I insisted on a start and at dusk we started, tied up with wire and rather tired. The driver was hopeless and it was a severe passage to Lagodekhi, but we got there eventually. It is a mainly Russian settlement, all tobacco; once there was a cavalry barracks there and boar were driven to the officers who stood in iron cages. We were quartered in an unattractive guest house, one storey with a verandah on which men sprawled and snored and talked and the wireless blared. The manager was a reasonable man, though the wrong shape. We were greeted by a dying Dane with a squint, who eagerly volunteered the information that he had been deported from Denmark and imprisoned by the British in Cairo for revolutionary activities. Drank some brandy in an amusing underground restaurant nearby. Mogs and I decided to sleep out at all costs, so wandered off with my sheepskin coat and her sleeping bag through the straggling village till we found a field. Here we fell asleep, to be awakened at sunrise by a furious and perplexed peasant. I must say if I found a couple of strange Russians sleeping on my lawn I should be a bit put out. I calmed him and we went our way, Mogs to sleep and I to sour milk in a cellar.

We were to start at 12 for the high tops and the *tours*.[1] We did in fact start at 2. Very hot winding up through

[1] The *tour* (*capra cylindricornis, Blutch*) is a mountain sheep of the moufflon type, whose habitat is the alpine pastures or the forests immediately below them.

the woods. I sweated a lot, being crammed with castor oil and things, but went very well. So I must say did Mogs. So did the two pack-horses. When the shadows were getting long we met a Lesgin, a jolly, effective-looking man, with a woman and a little boy tied on top of his horse's pack. From him we got the haunch of a *tour* he had shot and made *shashlik* of it. Awfully good. He said he would come up and shoot with us the next day. Then we went on. It was steep, the track was very bad, it was dark, and we were tired from the last few days. But at last we came out of the trees on to a high, bare spur, palely dotted in the moonlight with autumn crocuses. Big peaks all round and the world a long way below. It was like what perhaps it is like on the moon.

We went on and on, to camp at last on a sheep-trodden ledge where stood a semicircle of ruinous huts used by the shepherds in the summer.[1] The dirty cream-coloured horses looked as romantic as anything. We ate some soft-boiled eggs and drank some fine water and some brandy and lay down to sleep round a fire, George and Mogs in their little tent. Owls cried and the men made me come and drink with them. The chief is Daniel, manager of the local bank and president of the hunting society, a stooping man of some culture with a worried face and a good fur hat. Alexei, a red-haired brusque Russian, is a good one, and the best on the hill is an old, kind man exactly like all the tramps in *Punch*. Then there is a Turk with a huge bandolier, and Maxim.

I was up at 5. The full moon was still on the mountains, of which Hochal is the biggest and nearest, being about 9,000 feet. There was a little cloud in the valley. The men lay like headless black furry monsters in their

[1] See photograph between pp. 56–57.

burkas. Presently the dawn came and a wren sang some-where near. The camp woke up and made tea and Oxo, but the mist came up inexorably and for a bit we did not start. When we did start the day was a failure be-cause of the mist. We tried a *gai* [a drive], Alexei saw a *tour* but lost it, and after a lot of waiting about we got back to camp about 5, deciding to go down next day if it was no better. After our usual dinner of soft-boiled eggs, squashed, cold chicken covered with Georgian newsprint, and brandy, a little rain fell. I slept in a hut with the men, a fire like the mouth of hell burning at one end of it. They were very good to me and Alexei gave me his place when I got cold. About 1 a.m. Mogs and George came in, having been washed out of their tent by heavy rain, and we all slept in a pile in front of the furnace, Mogs looking very immature in the firelight.

Next day I was up early and saw a clear, lovely dawn with snow on the tops. We had some sort of breakfast and started at 8.15. Mist came down as we climbed up to the pass, where there is a spring, passing one or two blackgame on the way. We went east from there, and suddenly the mist lifted. We were in the next valley, looking down on it. The frontiers of Georgia, Azerbai-jan, and Daghestan all touch it. Two grinning fair-haired Lesgins with four man-eating dogs gave us sheep's milk which they were boiling over a muddy fire. We dropped down into the woods for a *gai*. It was fear-fully steep. Maxim, without climbing irons,[1] dropped less rapidly than we. We posted ourselves in dizzy, Dover-cliff vantage-points.

Nothing came of the drive, except a contemptuous

[1] Everyone else wore them. Some of the places were fairly precipitous.

white-headed eagle and a few somehow-different jays. But there had been shooting below us, and there was talk of thirty *tours* and a Russian party who had killed a little one. We dropped still further down and found this party sitting silently round a damp fire. It numbered 4—an introspective, frail, mouselike woman with huge eyes, in bulky, drab clothes and a bayonet, an effective boy called Peta, a man like a Scots stoker in a check cap, one very bloodshot bandit in a strange spiked cap who claimed to be the chauffeur from a sawmill in the valley. We ate some chicken and hunks of maize bread, then started mysterious preparations for a *gai* in conjunction with the other party. The woman faded away and I was told that she had gone to sleep.

As we were getting into position there was a whistle. Daniel and Peta looked in the wrong direction. I looked in the other and spotted three *tours* on a cliff opposite— yellow, exciting animals bounding perilously along the face. I was carrying two rifles, and had some delay giving Mogs hers, but got a quick shot at about 250 yards as the big one stood for a moment. I hit it, far back I expect, but they all went on, pursued by a *feu de joie* from Daniel and Peta, right round the corner and into the trees. The party reassembled and we had a halt while Peta did a very creditable climb up the cliff to look for tracks. But there were too many of these and the country round the corner was too bad to look further. So we gave it up. Very disappointing. To save the by now formidable climb we had sent a man back to our camp to take the horses and gear down to Lagodekhi, while we went on down our valley and got a car home from the sawmill at the bottom of it. The chauffeur talked a lot about this car.

71

The climb down was really stiff, breakneck glissading through wet leaves with plenty of brambles and rocks. It was also very long. But at last we hit the river bed. Down this we struggled for hours, the old tramp man showing a catlike agility in walking across fallen logs, for the river had to be forded about every half-mile. There were many tracks of *tour*, big stag, and bear. Mogs and George both had a long shot at a *tour* in an open scree above the river, but no luck. The going was awful and the leadership not first-class. It began to get dark and we should have had a bad time if we hadn't hit some sort of track with the last glimmer of light. We staggered on down this, past odd Lesgins encamped with wagons and buffaloes and fires, and reached the sawmill.

But here of course there was no car and no food, so we had to go on to a tobacco *sovhoz* [State farm] 3 km. further down. Here we lurched into a sort of office where a man was eating fruit. While he sent a horse into Lagodekhi for the car we made an astonishing meal, consisting in my case and in the following order of raw onions, pears, cheese, grapes, bread, sour sheep's milk, hot honey (the last two mixed), a bit of chicken and tomatoes in vinegar. Daniel, who was looking dead, got rather drunk on the knockdown grape vodka, which had however no effect on me. At 11.30 we took the road again—it was our fourteenth hour of hard going—and after about 2 km. met the car, had omelette and brandy in the cellar, and fell into bed. I have not had many harder days.

Slept from 2 till 6.30 and woke up feeling grand. But it was a typical day. We were to have started for a boar hunt at noon, and we did in fact get away at about

11.30 p.m. They are wonderful people. After endless changes of plan and roundings up it was decided that we should drive 12 km. into Azerbaijan in *kibitkas*, sit up by moonlight, and then have drives tomorrow. We were told to take no sleeping things. Mogs and I ran down the last *kibitka*—only it turned out to be no such thing, but a long open springless wagon—in a household deeply infected by melancholy. An old woman with a white cloth round her head wept angrily because her son, the driver, had had a bad fall while out after *tour* some time ago and was in her view in no state to spend the night out. But at last we clattered back in triumph to the hotel, where Boris had characteristically produced an ancient sort of victoria for the gentry. My God, we looked silly sitting up in it in state. We drove off shrieking with laughter to a rendezvous at somebody's house, where we ate some of our rations and were shown a fine *tour's* head by the Tramp. As we moved off, after more delay, somebody produced a fairly spirited chestnut stallion, which I seized the chance of riding.

We wound away in the moonlight, the victoria in the lead, two wagons, bristling with arms, rattling behind, and eight powerful dogs in full cry. We went through some woods where Maxim had shot a Lesgin bandit, and over the frontier into Azerbaijan, where more dogs dashed out at us from homesteads. The men in the wagons had a great joke about being the Chelyuskin expedition, and Cote being Schmidt. Mogs took the horse for a bit and darted about in the moonlight, making it do things. Then I got up again. It was like assisting at an elopement, riding beside the victoria in which Mogs's face was pale and George's hat was raffish. We

73

went for 4 hours, I in a strange numbed state past sleepiness, and at 3.30 a.m. halted in a plain. There was after all to be no sitting up for boar. The men lit some desultory fires of straw, then drank. I lay down in my sheep skin coat and slept warmly for two hours and a half.

By 6 we were trying to wake them up, which one of the drivers finally did. Beaters and dogs went off, while 6 guns scrambled hurriedly and at random through thicket after thicket, at last taking up in a murderous formation positions in dense cover which promised little to me. I was sleepy and unhopeful. But there was barking in the distance, and presently a jackal trotted past ten yards away. I killed it. After a little the sound of a motor bus coming through the undergrowth could be heard, and I saw, without believing, a monstrous boar trotting towards me 15 yards away. At 10 yards I fired and got it through the lungs. It came straight at me like a racehorse, then jinked. I had another quick hard shot and it vanished in the direction of George, going through the cover like a shell. It gave George no chance and was bearing down on Mogs, when she broke its hind legs with buck-shot in the 16-bore, and once more it vanished. Maxim marked it lying up in a thick place, and when we went into conference our voices scared it and it went off again. It left a lot of blood on its trail, and presently when the *gai* seemed more or less over a desultory and ill-organised pursuit started. In the end Maxim and I were left alone in the lead and came up with it. We could hear it making savage noises and struggling for breath in a terrifically thick place. We worked our way in gradually. I had left my rifle behind and my bogus bowie knife came in useful for clearing a

74

way through the thick cover. It was damned exciting.
At last we were very close. Maxim fired several shots at
the noise but missed, and we could hear it thrashing
about, trying to charge and occasionally making a great
lunge towards us. Still we could not see it. We worked
as a section, Maxim firing—sometimes misfiring—and
me giving him the knife when he wanted it and cutting
enough stuff to give us a chance of dodging if it did get
through and come for us. (It had been a good moment
when Maxim, seeing I had no rifle, had ordered me to
draw my knife.) At last we were right on top of it, but
still we could not see it and still it was trying to get at
us. (We didn't know the hind legs were broken.) Then
Maxim leaned right over and got a sight and put a
bullet into its head through the snout, and after one or
two filthy coughs it was still. We were both pouring with
sweat.

After that the day was rather anticlimax. With great
labour the boar was dragged out to a track. It looked to
me black and huge but apparently it was not a big one
as big ones go. Two Lesgins on horseback had unaccountably appeared in the middle of this impassable
jungle. We had two more drives, during which we
struggled to keep awake. Another jackal was shot and
its half-grown pup caught by the dogs. This had a bad
time, poor little thing. We did our best for it but I think
in the end they killed it for its skin. We had our first
meal of the day about 3.30. The boar *shashlik* was delicious. Then we said goodbye to the men who were staying out overnight and went back to Lagodekhi, getting
a pigeon and 2 pheasants en route. It was pleasant
country, with rather nursery-book little houses, hung
with gherkins and chiles and piled with pumpkins, the

orchards cropped short like lawns. The Azerbaijanese women were better looking and wore more colours than the Georgians. A lot had necklaces or belts of big silver coins. It took 4 hours. The horse was very dead by the end of it. The others, who were far in front, left a man with a face like a pantomime fiend to guide me through the wood where bandits were feared. We came slowly into Lagodekhi in the darkness, feeling that we had justified ourselves. After dinner when the others had gone to bed Cote gave me his views on the expedition. They adore Mogs and claim to like me, but can't make out George's way of speaking.

Through doing interpreter in camp my pidgin Russian is now pretty useful. It has been grand fun.

Got up at 6.30 next day. We were to have started at 9 for Tiflis. Finally got away at 11.30. Delay in a rainstorm for petrol, then crawled across a muddy plain to the other and more suburban side of the valley. At Gurdjani we had a bad lunch in a filthy, tawdry new eating-place, the measure, I suppose, of what all the Caucasus will be in time. In Telav we stuck again, hearing that a river had washed out the road and that we must take the 9.30 train. George and I played a game of billiards on a fantastic clothless table with polygonal balls, then Mogs and I started a game of battleships.

A terrific dinner was provided which I could not eat. Boris did bad imitations of us. Then we fought our way on to the train, which was unaccountably crowded, as though by refugees. We three commandeered a compartment which contained only a powerful woman with red hair who talked French and sang in her sleep. During the night I left Martin Lindsay's belt and my knife in the lavatory and they were pinched, so I was up a good deal, and watched the system of train-jumping which the people here have perfected to a fine art. The belt miraculously turned up again after I had given it up.

Got to Tiflis at 7. No car. Droshkied to the hotel, where George found that he had lost his knife and keys in the train. Mogs and I had an enormous breakfast beginning with caviar and cheese in my room, then went for a walk and had a heart-to-hearter. The Ogpu have found my haversack, which is an astonishing and undreamed-of slice of luck. The Gages go to Armenia probably tonight, I go to Baku tomorrow. I shall miss them sadly. They are damn good value and we have got on wonderfully. I am thin and in cracking good condition.

Wrote this up and saw the Gages off. Very sad.

THIRD STAGE

TO SAMARKAND

TO SAMARKAND

Packed and got off at noon, Boris with a terrific hang-over. My haversack returned minus torch and razor blades. Train slow, comfortable. Restaurant car filled with people from the stations we stopped at, drinking inconceivable quantities of beer. Boris got his usual three poods of grapes and a bottle of port-type wine of a puce colour. The usual extraordinary meal. Boris confided that the thing he found so difficult about the Gages was that they were always changing their plans; I knew it would be something hopelessly wide of the mark. He was also interesting about his time with the Jap M.A.[1]

Reached Baku at 2 a.m. Drove to the shoddy hotel, where the inevitable banquet was in full swing. Read until 4, then had nightmares.

OCTOBER 2

The Intourist manager, said to be a keen sportsman, is going to give me a shoot tonight. Saw the dreary town and the oil derricks in a car. The Caspian is like a flat grey stone better left unturned. Incautiously visited the Azerkino studios, where they showed me first a

[1] Boris, who I think was intermittently employed by the Ogpu, had been at one time interpreter to the Japanese Military Attaché in Moscow.

6   81

moderately effective documentary film of a gusher or whatever it is, then, my God, a film of an opera in Turki, featuring three characters, two pieces of scenery, and the orchestra. They were very nice chaps.

Baku a grimmish place, where there is said to be some feeling between the Turkis and the Russians. The shooting party, due to start at 11 p.m., left at 2.30 a.m., full of vodka and radishes, leaving its boasts hanging on the smoky air of the tasteless dining-room, where a funereal band played the tunes of my Hunt Ball days. I was very tired indeed, and still more so when at dawn, after traversing (in a car) a long but not particularly stiff point-to-point course, we stopped in a tufted desert, to which derricks stood sentinel, and waited for the little charabanc containing the rest of the party to turn up.

The first bout of antelope (*ghiran*) hunting was rather fun, the country being difficult and covered with tussocks, except in rare patches, which called for skill and strategy by the driver. We didn't get a shot at all, though the other party shot a huge vulture which they refused to finish off. We had some long points, bounding over the desert. One really ought to be strapped in. I slept a good bit in unlikely circumstances. There was a bit of rain, then a long halt at some *kolhoz* or other, during which I read a life of Peter Warlock, who must I think have been a tiresome man. The others at last rustled petrol and we went on parallel to the railway. Here we sighted two antelope and after a short, violent chase got one of them. It was no sort of fun, the ground being dead smooth and the beast having no chance. The driver was not taking chances, and instead of manœuvring for position made a stern chase of it. The whole thing was cruel and unsporting. I wrote some tart criticisms of these methods in their visitors' book afterwards.

Then we came to a village and had some desultory duck-flighting in a marsh with a lot of mosquitoes. There were quite a few duck but very few picked up. There seemed to be an extraordinary number of varieties. We came back to the village and quartered ourselves on a sinister-looking man who gave us a good room with carpets and coloured quilts on the floor. Here we had a meal with *shashlik*. I was awfully sleepy. They were good chaps to be with, though rather heavy. The guiding spirit was the Armenian, Aram, a very efficient and well-intentioned man. Then there were a fat, talkative man, a man who looked like an Irishman, and a very smart young man in a fawn-coloured suit. The gun they lent me was a German 12-bore, decorated like a Victorian sideboard. I still think there was a cuckoo clock somewhere among those carvings.

OCTOBER 3

Back to the marsh by dawn, having declined another antelope hunt. Poled through the reeds by villains in filthy dug-outs. Quite a lot of duck (at which I shot execrably) and some queer fowl, including what they call the Sultan's Chicken. Also unregarded snipe. Total bag 2 duck.

OCTOBER 4 (same day, but I have dropped a date somewhere)

The other party got 2 antelope, 2 foxes, and a stork. We breakfasted off grapes, sardines, and brandy. Then Aram and I caught a hard-class train, in which our antelope in a bag was much admired and in which we ate some crayfish. It took four and a half hours to reach Baku, and I feared that I should miss the boat which was due to sail at 4 p.m. But the boat, allegedly owing to a storm, was late, and did not in fact sail till 3.30 a.m. So I hung about and ate some rather irregular food and got on well with a malarial young Communist with protuberant eyes, who, as his wife very justly said, acted too grown up all the time. He was a nice chap. I seem to have gone down well here.

OCTOBER 5

The boat was a comic boat. The first thing that happened when I came on board was that the Captain asked me if I could possibly tell him the time. The lavatory key hung by the wireless in the saloon, but although everyone always took it with them the door was never locked. The doctor was a woman in a salmon-pink dress. The boat was a cargo boat, and they kept on excusing her deficiencies by pointing out that she was not meant to carry passengers. All the same she carried some 500, who lay in piles on the deck, eternally eating brown bread. The sea was blue and dead calm. I read *The Way of Revelation* by Wilfrid Ewart (of which the merits and the defects are implicit in the author's Christian name), and *Little Caesar* by W. R. Burnett, which was fun, and beat some half-witted Russians at chess. The day was blue and cloudless. The service and, I suspect, everything to do with the running of the ship was lousy. We got into Krasnovodsk at 10, too late to catch the train. We got permission to sleep on board, which we did, though they tried to turn us out at 3.

IN SAMARKAND

"TWO GUIDES AND SOME THREE-LEGGED HORSES" (p. 53)

A HEVSU

SANDINO SUMMONS ROSA (p. 64)

CONSTANTIN & CO. (p. 64)

"TO CAMP AT LAST ON A SHEEP-TRODDEN LEDGE" (p. 69)

"IT WAS FINE, WILD COUNTRY" (p. 54)

A HALT IN THE FOOTHILLS

STALIN'S BIRTHPLACE

"THIS VIOLENT DEMONIAC FIGURE"

"A GREAT WEARINE:

SAMARKAND: THE OLD CITY

TAMBURLAINE'S TOMB (p. 91)

STREET SCENE

"UZBEKS LOOK DOWN WITHOUT CURIOSITY" (p.

"...IKE SOMETHING OFF THE DUST-WRAPPER OF A THRILLER" (p. 93)

A TCHAIKHANA (p. 92)

"THE WRECKED TRAINS WE PASSED" (p. 101)

"JAPANESE SOLDIERS FIRING FROM UNDER THE WHEELS" (p. 121)

A PRAYER-WHEEL AT GANDJHUR

MONGOL GIRL

"WE PASSED A TROOP OF JAP CAVALRY" (p. 145)

"A CHARMING OLD MAN IN YELLOW" (p.

E UGURDA'S DAUGHTER-IN-LAW (p. 147)

A YURT

JEHOL: THE POTALA

MONGOL CAVALRY CHARGI

N THE SHORES OF LAKE KOKONOR (p. 189)

PÈRE CONARD

OCTOBER 6

Breakfasted on shore off two glasses of sour milk and a fish's head. Krasnovodsk is a small place, shut in by hills which are so spectacular that you think they are big until you see a gigantic human figure striding down them. Spent most of the disconsolate day in the waiting-room. Sanitary conditions worst I have ever come across; I do not seem to mind, however. The Kirghiz people the only compensation, with pleasant, surprised faces, very magnificent in their rags and fur hats, the women in their waisted coats.

In the afternoon I walked out of the town, through a cluster of round Kirghiz huts of furs and matting and anything you like, and over the biggest mountain to the sea. It was baking hot and dead still. The whole place is desert, without a blade of grass. On the sand and stones innumerable flies mysteriously pasture, rising with a buzz. On the shore I found men lying up in stone shelters for duck, an enterprise in which they were not assisted by a party of women and children who had chosen the same stretch of coast to bathe and wash their clothes. (There being no water here, I suppose the sea is the wash tub.) Eventually I bathed myself, a process which served the purposes of neither recreation nor hygiene, since the sea was only 6 inches deep and its floor of thick black mud. Still, it was better than nothing, though I got very dirty.

I walked back, and eventually found myself on a party in the stationary *wagon-lit* car of a railway chief from Ashkhabad, who gave me bad bortsch, some of Boris's sardines, and some wine. He was nice and probably able in a limited way. There were also present an irrigation expert, who declaimed one of his poems but forgot the last verse, a German-speaking commercial traveller, and the young manager of the Ash-etc theatre, a horrible youth.

The railway man told me that the Trans-Caspian Railway is fifty years old, pays its way, carries bread and oil in and fruit and cotton out, is going Diesel within five years on account of the water shortage, and is being double-tracked. Praised the Turksib with reservations.

After this the train appeared. The Moscow timetable said it left at 6.35, the station notice-board said 6.28, the latest rumours 6.18, and the railway chief, when consulted, 6.30. So I had plenty of time to go and buy some Borzhom [a staple brand of mineral water]. While I was doing this the train left suddenly at 6.22. I caught it at the gallop, giving Boris a nasty moment. We have got a soft-class compartment with two dim orthodox railwaymen on their way to some blithering conference. They are primed with dogma and not worth talking to. I went to sleep at 8, there being no light on the train and only 2 candles. The electrician has lost the driving belt and is under arrest. Made them leave the window open all night, as a result of which Boris has caught cold.

OCTOBER 7

Up very early. We are running along the bottom edge of the Kara Kum desert, with the hills of the Persian frontier close by to the south. It is very desolate country, with rare villages of round huts and black goats in the middle distance and some cotton and a good many camels and fur hats. I bought some eggs from an old woman but they were too soft-boiled. I am now living on Fortnum's and the country. Luckily the bread here is good. Books are getting low and tobacco very low. Boris very sorry for himself. Lovely day, air like hock. Compartment littered with grapes, unripe melons, empty bottles, cigarette ends, bits of bread, and oddments.

Desert changed as we went along, sometimes going Beau Geste, sometimes Sind. We had a bad quick meal at Ashkhabad, the capital of Turkmenistan, whose inhabitants are of the most picturesque. Living on the country makes it fun. One waits for each halt anxiously, hoping for milk, chickens, melons, grapes, bread, tomatoes, or mutton. Melons are the only safe bet. Vendors squat, or stand in a row. Some of the women wear a wonderful sort of top hat, with a snood or what-not hanging down behind. The men's fur hats are their strong point. I should love to show them a bearskin. Went to sleep early, spurning Boris's vodka substitute, which consisted of pure alcohol and some disgusting lemonade. The lavatories on this train are filthy, and it is hell using them at night, there being only one candle in the whole coach.

OCTOBER 8

We have turned a bit north and the frontier hills are gone. The desert continues to vary, but has not re-achieved its Caspian aridity. We crossed the Amu Darya, a wide, shallow, yellow river, the frontier between Turkmenistan and Uzbekistan. Ridiculous precautions were taken to keep the windows shut for fear of wrecking; the bridge seemed fairly heavily guarded, with a lot of barbed wire and some trenches which were probably relics of the civil war. I got some *kasha*, a form of porridge, at one place, and at Kagan, where the line branches for Bokhara, Stalinabad, and the Afghan frontier, we had a meal of which the best part was a mixture of sour milk and honey, my own invention.

During one stop there appeared out of the train a young Uzbek, half naked and of a singularly brutish aspect. He had the misfortune to be both demented and drunk. He reeled about among the shabby passengers and the magnificent locals, shouting, embracing, and stealing people's hats. Nobody did anything about him; this violent demoniac figure, whirling inconsequently in the sunlight, seemed to have a certain force and reality by comparison with the amiable and unprotesting Russians and the robed, impassive tribesmen. At last a great weariness came over him, and he lay down with his head on the rails down which an engine was approaching. When roused, he first crawled away like a dog, then made furious attempts to throw himself under the engine at the last moment. A reasonable-looking citizen restrained him with difficulty. The official apathy towards him (he was eventually detained at a station 2 hours later) contrasted with another place, where soldiers with swords and rifles were guarding two carriage loads of Turcomen who had been told that they were kulaks and were being deported to another part of the country. We also passed a troop train with a battalion (roughly) coming back from manœuvres. I watched the men drawing soup very noisily.

I had a Russian lesson from Boris with a big audience, then night fell. The whole train was now lit by only half a candle. The soft carriage is largely filled by delegates to this railway conference, and we had an impassioned commination of this line's inefficiency, for which their excuses were of the most feeble. They say of this, "It is an old railway, so you must not expect too much," and of the Turksib, "It is a new railway, so you must not expect too much." And so, 3 hours late, we reached Samarkand station, detrained, and got a very small droshky, in which, in exquisite discomfort under piles of luggage, we drove 7 km. into the city.

We drew up at a fine modern-looking hotel, but were told that owing to repairs in progress they had no rooms for us. After a bit of talk they thought they might manage to get us in, and put us in charge of a charming old servant who had married a Hungarian prisoner of war and had a daughter in Hungary and wished she was there too. She took us out to a restaurant (it was now about midnight) and here a fine fantastic scene ensued.

It was a small place, with horrid wallpaper and imitation lace curtains, and very full. A mixed lot were sitting round getting drunk on beer. A band of three played loudly. The pianist was a very sad woman with a bandage round her head. Our old lady said she hoped I didn't mind her saying so, but the girls at the other tables were all prostitutes. I who had been pitying them as poor seedy typists was surprised. The waiter said the restaurant had no food, as the cook was sick, but it turned out that the only thing they did have was sausages. All this way for sausages! They didn't seem bad at the time, with a good deal of vodka.

There suddenly appeared at our table a charming young Red Air Force lieutenant, who said he had mistaken us for some of the Chelyuskin fliers, alleged to be in town at present. He ordered food and drink for himself, offered me horses to ride and an aeroplane to

Tashkent. It was only when we left that I realised how drunk he was. In the street he drew an automatic and insisted on firing several salutes in honour of England. The old lady and I took an arm each and got him back to the hotel. When I came down from carrying some luggage upstairs I found the ugly blonde at the desk weeping convulsively, having been punched in the eye in her efforts to restrain him from shooting a lame man who had come in at that moment. We got the pistol away from him, and I took charge of it, repelling not without difficulty an assault on my room. It was fully cocked when I got it. This I discovered by firing it out of the window, thus increasing the alarm of my fellow guests. Slept like a hog. Filthily dirty.

OCTOBER 9

Autumn has suddenly come, if not winter. It is bright and cold and the leaves are beginning to fall. Samarkand is a good place. Breakfast in a little café where a kind man gave us eggs and very good bread and some sort of coffee. The lieutenant, whose name is Nikolai, was to be seen sitting in his room playing the gramophone and not much more than half conscious. In this state, smiling abstractedly, he took us to the bazaar, where I ordered a Red Army cavalry overcoat. There was a man very ill or very drunk, covered with blood, sitting about in the street and being convulsed. Nobody took any notice of him. A cavalry regiment rode past, some of the officers on good horses, part Arab. One man in each troop of about twenty carries an automatic rifle, and they have machine-gun units with the guns on horses. They looked a likely lot. Then I saw a military funeral, with a band, and the corpse in an open coffin, and a small cavalry escort leading his charger and laughing a good deal.

We fought our way into some kind of bus and went to the old city, a fine place. We found a guide in El Registan, a square surrounded on three sides by huge broken blue-mosaicked buildings and leaning tubular towers, from the top of one of which criminals used to be thrown. A certain amount of restoration going on. Then we went through narrow, pleasant, rather villagey streets to Tamburlaine's tomb. It has a big cupola, fast going bald of blue tiles. Outside it was a pond and a bit of open space, very like a village green. A very old foolish man, who lives in the tomb with the magpies, showed us round. First of all there is a sort of chapel, with coffin-like stones commemorating Tamburlaine, his military teacher, his son the astronomer, his minister and another son. Tamburlaine's is a fine thing of dark green stone from China called nephritis (?). Two long sort of pikes, with dark green banners and tufts of some *ovis* fur hanging from them, stand over the military teacher's tomb. Then you go down into the vaults by a sinister stairway. They are brick and today very warm. The brickwork looks oddly new. Here are the tombs proper, the same sort of coffin-like slabs, and the passage through which they carried Tamburlaine in and which they then walled up.

After that we went back through El Registan, where from a doddering bearded professor I procured in time a complicated form authorising me to take photographs, and on to the palace of Tamburlaine's wife, Bibi Khanum. This is highly ruinous, the last damage having been done by an earthquake only 28 years ago. There are little patches of maize and sunflower cultivated in the place, and among them stands the huge lectern on which the Koran was placed. We went on to the outskirts of the city, where is Shah-Zindeh. It is a very holy place, or was, and looks like a fortress. A lot of Tamburlaine's family are buried in little mosque-like shrines, with some fine mosaic work. The huge Koran, allegedly written by the Prophet's secretary, is kept in a wooden cage. Beside it there was a little sort of cell, containing some splendid *ovis* heads left by the devout and another of those pikes, to which women tie coloured rags, I think when they want children. Then we came back, Boris going very short, and had delicious pilaffe in a *tchaikhana* [tea-house].[1] Drinking was not allowed there, and we had to bootleg our vodka and drink out of bowls.

It was now freezing hard, and I walked back at full speed, leaving Boris to follow. In the hotel we had a heart-to-hearter, he telling me all about his son and his difficulty in reconciling a good Communist's attitude towards the family with his own instinctive one. Finally we adjourned to the place we were in last night and talked there for a long time. He told me that from his point of view the bad thing about me was that I never got tired. We had a long argument about Mogs's alleged sentimentality about the horses at Passanour.

Nikolai still claims to be able to fly me to Tashkent, but I fear nothing will come of it.

OCTOBER 10

Thwarted at the railway bureau, so took a droshky with a fiendish driver to the station, where we fixed up about tickets. I walked the five miles back and got

[1] See photograph.

warm. Boris feels the cold terribly, though it is not much. The colours of the people's clothes are wonderful. Quilted or fur-lined coats striped and patterned in good rich colours. Men squatting on small long-eared donkeys, which they guide with a stick, lead their two or three camels. Carters sit on a saddle with their feet on the shafts. Everybody eating grapes. Good hats and caps. Many of the women wear black veils, which is probably a good thing and makes them look like something off the dust-wrapper of a thriller.[1] Lot of trees in the streets, and water running in deep gutters.

Boris in very bad form, so left him and went to the Old City again. Once more guzzled pilaffe, then wandered round. More going on, because earlier. Carts with six-foot wheels. A procession of children being harangued and carrying anti-Nazi caricatures on cardboard. Uzbeks passing on their raffish horses look down on the procession without curiosity.[1] An old man selling gourds talks to another; the other takes a live quail out of his long padded sleeve and they both examine it with an amused yet professional air. Everybody is selling something, or else taking a long time to buy it. The veiled women have a somehow helpless look, like balloons. In one place some not very impressive handmade coloured stuffs are offered. The horse market is empty. It was a good drifting afternoon. Walked back and packed and received my Red Army overcoat, which is fine and makes me look like a cross between Rupert of Hentzau and Lot's Wife.

Nikolai had promised us his lorry at 6 to catch the train at 8, but of course it didn't turn up, and about 6.45 I made Boris put the luggage in a droshky and set

[1] See photograph.

out on foot myself. After stumbling in the dark for about two miles I was suddenly picked up by Nikolai, who was beaming with delight at the lorry having come to save his face. We had a meal with him and his driver in the station, failing to do justice to two gallons or so of disgusting beer which he kindly ordered. Then we boarded the train, on which we shared a compartment with an old bearded disconsolate oaf who had lost the straps of his luggage. The most irresolute of men, he mooned in and out of the carriage like an unhappy bear. He gave a whimper of delight when I found the straps on my bunk just above his head. He was somehow an appealing figure. The other occupant was a noncommittal young man.

OCTOBER 11

Reached Tashkent with snow mountains, the Altai, to be seen, early and spent a rather foolish day there. Boris was almost speechless and in very very bad form. We took a tram to what he believed to be the centre of the city, but the centre of the city turned out to have moved since his day, and for a long time we wandered about looking for a restaurant. When it finally seemed beyond question that no restaurants were open yet, we had a still drearier and not less fruitless quest for the irrigation expert,[1] but when we did find his headquarters they too turned out to have shifted. So we took another tram down to the Old City, a long way off, and

---

[1] Looking for, and not finding, an irrigation expert was the sort of thing one constantly found oneself doing in Russia. I have completely forgotten what we wanted to see this one for; certainly it was nothing to do with irrigation. He may have been the man who recited poetry at Krasnovodsk.

there at last, when it seemed that Boris was going to die at any moment, we found in the bazaar a place in the open where they were selling food.

We had a bowl of moderate pilaffe, on a small rock in which I broke one of my teeth. I told Boris to go and find a doctor for himself and hung about the bazaar for a bit. The whole place is shoddier and more modern than Samarkand. I sat in the sun and watched the people and cursed my ignorance. Took a tram back to the station and found Boris slightly better but apathetic, so for the rest of the day we did nothing but hang about, varying this with the usual maddening expedition to Torgsin for a kettle. It took us an hour to buy one, very nearly. Said farewell to civilisation with a meal of tepid meat and bad port wine and caught the Turksib train at 7.30. For some reason it started 20 minutes late, and spent the first 3 hours of its run mostly standing still. The Turksib proper begins at Lugovaya.

TO VLADIVOSTOK

TO VLADIVOSTOK

OCTOBER 12–15 (on the Turksib)

An unexpectedly good run. The coach was better kept than on the Trans-Caspian, but the compartment was less good. The berths were shelves padded rather more than less and equipped with a deafening creak and the better—quantitatively speaking—part of a sheet. Mine I tore in two and used for washing up. This was regarded by the Russians as a considerable piece of daredevilry. The first two nights, as far as Alma Ata, we had with us a small blonde, reasonably pretty and a nice person, and a very base man who spoke French and claimed to be an official from Tiflis. This horrid fellow organised a party on the first day, playing some of his records on my gramophone and plying everyone with vodka, mostly ours. A lot of *tamada* stuff and old Georgian hospitality. A handsome brunette from along the corridor came in, and an informal dance was held, Boris displaying great enthusiasm and an ultra-Hammersmith style. It was great fun, and when at length it ceased to be I retired to my berth. This at no time easy manœuvre was rendered unusually difficult by the presence of four people and the vodka I had drunk. When I swung myself up I kicked the case of gramophone records and broke 4. This was very sad, but I must say I was surprised when the next morning our genial host asked me to pay for 2 of them. I told the

indignant Boris to give him a little valuta and retaliated
only with a good deal of eyebrow-lifting. Afterwards,
when I discovered that he had pinched most of my
needles, I wished I had reacted more definitely. He was
a loathsome little man.

He and the blonde left us at Alma Ata, a very hill-
station sort of place under the white mountains. Before
you get to it—somewhere on the first day—there is a
tunnel I should say about half a mile long. I seem to
remember it being featured in the film.[1] After that we
had the brunette in with us. She was very nice and did
housekeeper quite well, counteracting Boris's pro-litter
tendencies and mending my coat. For me she conceived
a passion which she declared through Boris. For 3 days
I was compelled to keep up an elaborate mock-flirta-
tion, based on the assumption that she was going to
desert her husband in Novosibirsk and come on to
Vladivostok with me. It was only a moderately amusing
game but it helped to pass the time. Boris, however, was
rather jealous and his throat had a relapse whenever she
gave him some tender nothings to translate. Her name
was Nonna, she had been married since she was sixteen,
she had one son, she worked as a stenographer for
Kuzbaz, she was cheerful like a sparrow, she had sense
and some character, she was highly romantic and was
observed to weep over the last chapter of a torn book
which she described as dealing with the tragedy of a
feminine soul, she was very kind to me and constantly
pressed food on me, she made the most of herself; she is
probably best summed up as a good trouper. She had a
lot of very bad, slightly disreputable stories, mostly

[1] A documentary dealing with the construction of the Turksib
had been shown outside Russia a year or two earlier.

about Jews. We parted with regret at Novosibirsk under the eye of her husband, from whom Boris was trying to borrow some roubles.

The fourth berth was occupied at one time or another by three men, of whom the most memorable was the Commissar, a ragged, dirty, cheerful shepherd from a big state-farm in the hills near the Turkestan border. He blew in out of the night at a very wayside station, grinning. He had a bottle of vodka with him and was going to Semipalatinsk on 12 days' drinking leave. He had served under Kolchak, and some of his family who had also done so lived now in England, a country for which he professed an admiration. He said that the point about Kolchak was that his intriguing staff let him down. He was a nice chap.

Then there was a nice, rather vague railway inspector in a fur hat, who didn't seem to know much about the railway but said they weren't going to double-track it, that it paid its expenses, that a lot of the northward freight trains were run empty, and that the wrecked trains we passed—mostly oil—had been due to the rails getting loose.[1] Finally there was a very sour-looking man, also in a fur hat, who was taciturn and seemingly on the point of tears.

Mountains were always in sight to the eastward for the first two days. There was a little snow on the higher parts of the line. The first day there were a lot of poplars. The second day we crossed the Ili and in the afternoon did a very long, slow, zigzag climb up what looked quite a gentle slope; then a rather good bit through sort of gorges where we were obstructed by a cow. The third day was all steppe and pretty foodless. Especially

[1] See photograph opposite p. 112.

towards the end, there were new buildings going up at even the smallest stations. On the evening of the third day we reached Semipalatinsk, crossed the Ob, and were all too clearly in Siberia. The familiar wells, which are called storks, and black mud, and bigger horses, and distances which are empty without being a desert. On the Turksib the Kazaks are said to work well. The country was all dun. Very well watered. I think the railway is certain to open it up in time. Some oil is said to have been located somewhere near the line.

Food was fairly plentiful [at the stations: there was of course no dining car], and I kept most of my supplies in reserve. (How the packing and the tins are admired when produced. These people are just like Carajas [an aboriginal tribe in the interior of Brazil]; you'd think they had never see a decent tin, and you wouldn't be far wrong.) I was once reduced to raw onions, but there were often milk, eggs, bread, gherkins, melons, grapes, potato cakes, etc. We got a bottle of bad port at one place. The buffets were always crowded and badly run. Inside the one at Alma Ata there was a house-martin without a tail flying about. Not many troops about anywhere on the line. Frontier said to be very closely guarded. One very good dish of sheep's milk, cheese, and sugar. Siberia flowed with milk and honey from the word go. But it was depressing getting back to the grain elevators and civilisation.

OCTOBER 15

At Barnaul they told us there was a Vladivostok express leaving Novosibirsk at 10 that night. So we were delighted when our train arrived, very nearly punctually, at Novosibirsk at dusk. It would have been still more punctual, only the engine couldn't quite manage the steep run-in, and had several times to *reculer pour mieux sauter*, like a drunk man failing to mount his own doorsteps.

Novosibirsk seems to me a pretty ridiculous place. First of all they told us the alleged train didn't exist. Then there were no porters. Three successive officials came up and ticked us off for leaving our luggage on the platform, and the highest of these was prevailed on to provide us with the means of moving it. In the meantime the *provodnik's* [sleeping-car attendant] son had reluctantly declined to help us move it 10 yards out of the way, on the ground that, although there were no porters, it was against regulations for him to usurp their office.[1] Finally we got a droshky (which was in the process of being moved on by the police) and drove to the Central Hotel, an imposing modern building.

Here they wouldn't let us have a room until we had been disinfected. So while our clothes were baked we had a hot shower-bath with another victim, a little man like a pig, then sat in a sort of office in loincloths, trying to persuade a bovine blonde to take our clothes out of the oven before the regulation half-hour. This she refused to do, but at last it was over and we were dressed and had our certificates of cleanliness. It took about an hour and a half.

When we had paid in advance for the bad and dirty rooms we had no Russian money left. So we found our way to Insnab, a restaurant for foreign workers

[1] A British traveller in the 1950's might not have bothered to comment on what he would have been trained to recognise as a normal assertion of one of the tenets of Trades Unionism.

where everyone said they would take valuta. But they wouldn't, and we finally had to pay the bill by depositing dollars and promising to come and redeem them tomorrow. Here we had a meal of nauseous caviar, tough ram's meat, and a huge, delicious, sickly slice of cake, washed down with vodka. A German and an American, both pretty silly-looking people, were having an earnest conversation about a sprocket at another table. Several Russians were drinking beer. A red banner propounded Communistic sentiments in German. A band came in and played later on. It was a dowdy place, full of cockroaches.

OCTOBER 16

Got up early and walked round the city for 2 hours. It is full of gigantic buildings, very modern and flattered by the autumn sunshine. They are separated from each other by sloughs of black mud, only the main streets being roughly metalled. There is a lot in the windows of the shops, and at least two Torgsin kiosks, new to me.

The Siberians have learnt that depressing early-morning bustle of the office-goer. Some good horses. Boris had a blind last night with his room-mate, a disgruntled engineer, and got into action late. But we got the money from the Post Office and went in search of breakfast. The chief restaurant was shut as they were having a meeting. At the other one they made Boris leave his cap and coat upstairs, in spite of the fact that he was only half dressed underneath. Then he went to get the tickets and change £5 for a very small number of dollars. Tried to buy tobacco in Torgsin but failed as they had no change.

Then we went to a film called *Nastenka Something* and supposed to be good. It was lousy and even to Boris incomprehensible. As soon as a rape or a suicide was about to take place they inserted an inexplicable sequence of a train rushing along. Much of the acting was bad and none distinguished. The lighting was bum, the propaganda sickly. "The negro Root" figured in the cast, but was seen only once, leading a jazz-band in a parody of New York night-life. The capitalist, degraded by the revolution, attempted to wreck the Soviet régime by putting vinegar on his former coachman's sore leg to prevent the fellow from going to apply for work. The woman in the title rôle had a face like a horse and was very blowsy. The whole thing was a bad job of work. It ended with the converted foreign expert being given a car.

It was, however, preceded by a very good cartoon, a direct crib of Disney, and the only real bit of humour I have found in Russia. The hero was the hedgehog Yush (or Yosh). He was seen driving a train. There was one lavatory joke. Then we had a meal in the now open restaurant, where some dingy, ugly tarts danced with each other, wearing their clothes like little girls dressed up as adults. We got to the station at 6.15, my train being due at 8. It arrived at 11.30, Boris in the meantime having left for Moscow, hard-class, on a very full train. Poor Boris, he did very well by me on the whole. I think he liked me.[1]

[1] I used to write to Boris for a time, but I never got an answer. In 1937, finding myself once more in Moscow, I enquired for him at Intourist's head office, where they said they had never heard of such a person. I doubt if he survived the purge in which, at this period, several millions of Soviet citizens lost their lives or what passes for their liberty.

105

It was lovely getting on the Trans-Siberian express —real luxury. I had a mild railway official in my compartment, which is good but not of the best kind; but he left in the middle of the night and now I am alone. I feel very pleased with complete solitude, the first for some time.

Also waiting in the station were some Chinese from the Novosibirsk Consulate, mostly Southern and all very dapper. We had some laughs, as between civilised people. There was a Leningrad professor on his way from Kamchatka to the Pamirs. He was a geologist, an intelligent man who had had something to do with the Chelyuskin rescues. He told me some very interesting stuff which I will type when we are stationary.

Later. The Chukchy people [the aboriginal population of a peninsula which forms, so to speak, the top right-hand corner of Siberia]. About 18,000; 15,000 nomads and 3,000 sea Chukchys—25% of the latter are half-breeds, owing to American, Norwegian, etc., sailors. They think their blood is weak and will offer you their women to improve the stock. Controlled by frontier guards. Nominally local Soviets. All have Winchesters. Old men ask to be killed. This illegal, but still done; they have a party, then a young man strangles him. Don't bury their dead, but leave them out with all necessary possessions. Some of the half-breeds due to exiles from the Caucasus. Villages from two to fifty *yarangas*. The back room in these is so hot that all sleep naked. Like the Carajas, the women speak a different language; the male letter R is the female TS. *Yaranga* frames made of whale ribs. Count by hands. Word for *Twenty* same as the word for *Man*. Will steal alcohol but nothing else. Disapprove of Europeans for bringing firewater and diseases. Use some English words, like *whisky* and *captain*. Religion shamanism, partly animism. Each branch has its totem animal. Very weak heads. Never wash. Twelve dogs to a sleigh. Feed them on walrus. Know reindeer only as food. Officially monogamous.

The Arctic sea route [connecting the North Sea with the Pacific] is open only from July 30 to Sept. 20. And that only by dint of meteorological stations equipped with several aeroplanes and every sort of specialist. There are about fifteen [1] in the Chukchy area.

OCTOBER 17

Marmalade for breakfast. All bridges are double bridges, except over the Yenisei at Krasnoyask and, I think, the Oka at Isem. The train is several hours late. The leaves are off the trees. The silver birches look slim and supplicating. One guard with fixed bayonet covering the train on a bridge. Had a woman and child in my compartment all the afternoon. Rather sweet. Tremendous lot on sale at stations. Milk, butter, potato cakes, chickens, every sort of thing. Train staff very nice. At Krasnoyask I got in the compartment a young (32) flying officer, very cheerful and blue-eyed. We had a late party in the dining-car, with some dowdy girls, with the most sinister of whom I had an unsolicited success. A bad gramophone and some impossible dancing. There is an Intourist lady on her way back from escorting the crook P—— (Mukden, 1931) to Moscow. She is slow-witted and a bad interpreter and has never

[1] Fifteen meteorological stations? Fifteen aeroplanes? Fifteen specialists? We shall never know.

heard of Shakespeare. She organised General Post and a game in which you had to answer the questions put to other people. I didn't know what they were, but stuck to *Nichevo* and *Sechas* and proved my theory that these are the only two words you need.[1]

Just passed a train with many lorries, some Red Cross carts, and a dozen small tanks. Lorries without bodies. Sing Ho for Oppenheim!

OCTOBER 18–24 (Amur Railway to Vladivostok)

Not much to tell of these days. I got a lift on the engine round Lake Baikal through a young journalist.[2] It was good romantic stuff with a full moon and tunnels like a scenic railway at Wembley. Another train popped out of one like a plumed monster in the moonlight. In

[1] *Nichevo*, as everybody knows, means "Never mind, it doesn't matter." *Sechas* means "Instantly, now, this very moment," and is the answer automatically and often very charmingly given to all questions about the time at which some expected, hoped-for, or scheduled event will in fact occur. It may perhaps be called the Slav equivalent of *mañana*, for it offers an estimate of delay which, though less defeatist, is liable to be equally misleading.

[2] The Trans-Siberian Railway skirts the southern shore of Lake Baikal, the largest freshwater lake in the Old World (see map). The construction of the original permanent way involved the making of (I think) some 40 tunnels in the cliff. When the railway was double-tracked the second track had in some cases to by-pass the existing tunnel on a permanent way built out over the waters of the lake. Since these diversions would probably affect the vulnerability of the line to air attack in the event of a second Russo-Japanese War (at that time a possibility) I wanted to know roughly how many of them there were. In autumn, with all the compartment windows shut, it would have been difficult to obtain this information from inside the train, and impossible to obtain it without being taken for some sort of spy. It was easy if you travelled on the engine-driver's cab.

the cab it was hot and very dirty. The three men were agreeable. The engine-driver sat staring out of the window and finally went to sleep.

The next night we reached Chita. From there on the women at the stations had next to nothing to sell, a great contrast to the riches of Siberia. The line was like a prolonged lumber camp, work going forward furiously but sporadically and mostly being done by prisoners, though there were few guards in sight. I expect only the best characters are allowed to work on the line itself. A little snow lay dirtily under the bare and desolate trees. As you go east the country gradually mollifies itself. Gets flatter, with brush instead of woods. Finally from Habarovsk on it is docile and cultivated.

I got very bored. A succession of rather stolid Red Army officers shared my compartment. The train staff were particularly nice. A maddening girl from Intourist used to badger me a bit. Very dogmatic about English institutions: I pulled her leg gloomily, from a sense of duty. In one station in the buffet they had pictures showing how to get the better of tanks and a detailed diagram of a Japanese infantry section dug in behind wire. Not many soldiers to be seen. Aeroplanes the last part of the way. The Intourist girl took me for a spy and clumsily angled for the cover of the American edition of *Brazilian Adventure* and thus for my dossier.

At last reached Vladivostok, only about 12 hours late. Met *en prince* by the entire staff of Intourist and got my first mail for 2 months and my first bath for 3 weeks. Then dined very well with the manager and his assistant, a charming young man from Manchuria. After dinner we went to a genteel night resort run by Intourist for the benefit of visitant sea-captains. To two of these who were English I spoke. They commented on the plethora of submarines in these parts.

Last year there was a shortage of most things here, the line being monopolised by the military. But now they can get anything. Lot of vague hunting plans discussed. On the strength of a letter from Moscow, who ought to have known better, they have paid 3,000 roubles to the Fur Trust to look out for tigers, and think of my hunt in terms of weeks. I have disillusioned them.[1]

OCTOBER 24

Very cold. Sporadic vicious snow. Nothing much doing. Spent the afternoon talking to the head of the Fur Trust, a large, specious man, about hunting, finally deciding that it would cost too much and take too long. Then saw Watanabe, the Jap Consul, who was charming though discursive and gave me fruit when I went away. The interesting things he said were that Blucher [2] is not at all independent; that some of the officers, especially the marines, in Vladivostok are treating the

[1] While in Moscow I had expressed a keen desire to try for a Siberian tiger during the week or so which I knew I would have to spend in Vladivostok waiting for a sea-passage to Korea. I did not seriously expect anything to come of this; but my passion for shooting—a perfectly genuine one, as the reader will probably have noticed—seemed a useful ticket on which to try to travel in areas to which foreigners were normally denied access.

The Siberian tiger (*Panthera tigris longipilis*) is the biggest of the tigers; its fur is longer and paler in colour than that of other species. It is found in parts of Eastern Siberia, Manchuria, and North Korea. A pair I had seen in the Moscow zoo quite dwarfed their next-door neighbours from Bengal.

[2] Then Commander-in-Chief of the Far Eastern Red Army. Long since believed to have fallen from grace and been liquidated.

civilians cavalierly; that there is no racial feeling, even in times of ferment; and that Litvinoff had left an opening for Russia to recognise Manchukuo.

I walked about in the wind a bit, then went to the theatre with the Intourist brunette. A lousy farce, acted without distinction on a grubby stage, about a girl who pretends she is going to have a baby. Very long. Then we had a heavy supper at the hotel and the band played *Tipperary* and got a dollar. The girl is quite nice but hard work. She comes from Harbin and means to enter the diplomatic service.

OCTOBER 25

Typical Russian day. Breakfast at 11.30. Then told I must go and report at once to the N.K.D. [the local branch of the Commissariat of Foreign Affairs]. Meanwhile plans have been changed and a hunting expedition is proposed with me, one of the Japanese, and two film men, to cost me £20 and last ten days. Starting tonight. Tickets bought, medicine bought, food collected. But for two hours no car comes, so we hang about. Finally we get to the fur place and fix it up with endless talk. (No telephoning is possible today, as they have just switched over to an automatic system and nobody knows anybody's number.) We are held up at the fur place because the (quite unnecessary) car has disappeared. At last the manager turns up and says that the train, for which we bought the tickets this morning, is not tonight but tomorrow. The whole thing sounds to me like a bad bet but is too fantastic to miss and I can't get out of here anyway.[1]

[1] My boat for Korea was not due to sail until several days later.

THE REST OF OCTOBER

My God, it *was* a bad bet. After a pleasant lunch with the Japanese Consul we started off at 8 p.m. on the train. Krasavtsev and the irrelevant and gluttonous Alexei from Intourist, the charming Mimura from the Japanese Consulate, and a huge, handsome cameraman from Moskino. This was on the 26th. The hunter from the fur company didn't turn up at all, though we had bought his ticket. No one seemed surprised.

Here are some notes I made on the following day:

Oct. 27. Due at Iman 5.50. Mimura and I all set to leave the train at 5.30. Arrive Iman 8.30.

10 a.m. News comes that we have been promised two cars, a splendid chauffeur, and a good road by the general in command.[1] But we shall want a tent, perhaps. So Krasavtsev and I go back to the general, who is busy. We are sent to the local Soviet. By the head of this we are promised one car and good rifles immediately.

11.30. The O.C. transport appears and says that the chauffeur is very tired but the car will be here in half an hour.

1 p.m. A man is told to telephone to the local Soviet and find out what has happened to the car.

1.30. A search-party is sent out to look for this man, who instead of telephoning from the station walked to the Post Office and telephoned from there to the local Soviet, which is next door to it. He got no reply.

1.40. It is getting cold sitting on our luggage. We decide to have lunch. But the buffet is closed. We are told that it will be open in five minutes.

[1] We were a rather surprisingly constituted party to be allowed into the heavily fortified frontier zone along the Ussuri River.

2.10. Entry into buffet effected with the help of the railway police.

2.25. Lorry driver appears. Panic in buffet. Food gulped down.

2.30. We dash out of buffet. Lorry has disappeared, to get a few more military permits.

3.0. Lorry reappears. But man in charge of baggage room is busy and cannot attend to us.

3.10. Railway police force him to attend to us.

3.20. The lorry has been loaded at top speed. We take our places. But Krasavtsev, suddenly remembering the promised rifles, disappears.

4.0 Krasavtsev reappears. Plans entirely changed. Lorry unloaded. There is said to be a tiger 30 km. from Byasemskaya, further up the line. We shall catch the 5 o'clock train.

6.0. We catch it. We are due at midnight.

3 a.m. We arrive and go to sleep on the floor of the buffet.

I did not sleep but sat staring at the incalculable fools who haunted the buffet, none could say why. When it got light we had breakfast and Krasavtsev and I went to the local Soviet. Here we waited for an hour and a half, until a man came and talked a good deal of specious nonsense and promised to help us. But today is Sunday and no hunter can be fetched before nightfall. Eventually we will proceed by a light railway to an alleged lumber camp. In the meantime we can have a hunt near the village.

At this point I regretfully tell the nice Krasavtsev that I am going back to Vladivostok, as all this is not good enough and I want to catch the boat for Seishin [in Korea: now called Chongjin] on the 30th. In the afternoon we carry our own luggage some way through the mud to the house of a pleasant family, full of sauerkraut and one or two ikons and lots of family photographs. Then we go out with a fairly effective man to shoot. There is of course nothing to shoot, but in lovely country patchily covered with snow we try our rifles. These are very old, very dirty army rifles. Of three, one will not fire at all, one fires by itself whenever you push the bolt in, and the other at least goes off. We splodge home through the mud, Krasavtsev laming himself in his new boots. We eat a lot of our provisions, which include God knows how many kilograms of jam and 40 litres of alcoholic refreshment. Night falls and the hunter comes, a cherubic old abstainer with some humour and the usual immensely plausible air. Funny stories are told. All Russian funny stories are very bad. We hear that a road from Vladivostok to Habarovsk will shortly be completed, and Mimura pricks up his ears. I go to sleep at table.

At 12.30 a.m. they wake me up. I stagger through the mud with my luggage and go to sleep in the buffet. At 3.30 my train arrives and an imbecile railway official puts me in the wrong carriage. I have to sleep on the narrow shelf intended for luggage and backed by the hot-water pipes. I have some tinned things but no liquid of any kind. The carriage is crammed with dreary women and seedy Chinese. In the morning everyone is rather disagreeable. But at last I am befriended by a nice young journalist, who gets me into the right carriage, which is the same one we travelled up by. The women *provodniks* are kind to me. There are three very big officers poring silently over maps and writing. They keep themselves to themselves. In the afternoon I sleep. I wake up to find that a cheerful blonde girl on the bench opposite has hurt her foot badly. At Iman she got on to the wrong train and jumped off it after 2 or 3 kilometres. I promise her the car which is going to meet me at Vladivostok tomorrow. I read Boswell and play a little chess with a bloody man, and eat some sardines. At 1 a.m. I go to sleep.

At 6.30 we arrive; there is no car. The lame girl is carried to the waiting-room. I walk to the hotel, carrying my luggage. The wire announcing me has not come. After an argument with a drunken Swede I get the car, go back to the station, and find the wretched girl has gone in a tram. I go back and have a bath and a man takes my passport to buy my ticket. The boat for Korea will sail at 3 p.m.

Then I discover that my despatch case is open, and the money that I thought I had is gone. I ask the manager, Medvedev, if he will take a cheque. He says no. There is a good deal of coldness. It is now 1 o'clock and the only thing to do is to try and borrow from the Japanese Consul. So I ask what my bill comes to. They say 160 gold roubles. They are charging me the full £20, having failed to supply any of the services they promised for it. There is an Ugly Scene, out of which (in my opinion) Medvedev comes pretty badly (and throughout which there lies on his table a pamphlet entitled *The Determination of Hydrocyanic Acid in White Clover*). But time is short and I can do nothing. I gallop to the Consul, who is in the middle of a lunch party. He very kindly undertakes to guarantee payment. I go back. Just as the car is about to take me to the boat they discover that the exit visa which they said they had got me for both Pogranichnaya and Vladivostok applies only to the former.[1]

Panic. Medvedev reluctantly, hating me, goes to the officials. I go to the boat and the Consul does what he can. But it is a free day,[2] and in the end they cannot find the man who signed the visa and the boat sails without me. I must wait two days and go by train to Harbin, where I don't want to go and which is more expensive. By this time I am just about numb. I feel that Intourist have plumbed the depths of inefficiency. But no; they contrive to leave my luggage in the shipping office, so that I have only a typewriter to sleep in.

In the hotel I find a vain, blowsy, but intelligent Russo-American singer, who is interesting about the army and navy, to whom he is giving concerts. He has a blonde, sensible Scots wife and a disillusioned American girl with him. They all hate Intourist. At dinner, thank God, I find the sea-captain of a few nights ago. He comes from the Orkneys and thinks he has heard Martin Lindsay describing his Greenland expedition on the wireless, which is grand news if it is true. He keeps me sane, though only just.

[1] Pogranichnaya is the point at which the railway running west from Vladivostok crosses the Manchurian frontier. In those days, and I imagine also in these, the Russian authorities demanded, before granting an entry visa, that the traveller should specify the place at which he proposed to leave Russian territory at the end of the period for which his visa was valid. Knowing, when I applied for my visa in London, that ships sailed rarely and irregularly to Korea from Vladivostok, and knowing also that by the time I reached Vladivostok my visa would be near its date of expiry, I had (as I thought) arranged things so that I could leave by rail if no ship was available.

[2] A free day is the equivalent, *mutatis mutandis*, of Sunday.

TO VLADIVOSTOK

I hadn't had all that was coming to me. After a dreary day yesterday, relieved only by writing a fizzing letter to Moscow and a crack with the American girl, who has come here to study music and seems enterprising, I went to bed for a few hours. At 3.30 a.m. I got up in plenty of time to catch my train and had a long talk to the girl Shura, who suddenly came and was very nice. Then I went to the station with the disgruntled little agent who had bought my ticket and done what he could for me. Then, by God, what should we find but that the train for which they had sold me a ticket didn't exist. There was no through train to Harbin, only to Grodekovo [on the Russian side of the Manchurian frontier]. Still, that was better than nothing, and I set off in a hard-class carriage feeling glad that now at least there would be scope for action and enterprise and that I was free from Intourist.

The journey took 7 hours. At Nikolsk I got some milk for some cents, but having no roubles [1] I couldn't manage a meal. At the frontier I was received with grave suspicion. They said that I couldn't stay the night there without a special pass. The only thing to do was to go back to Vladivostok on the train from Harbin, which really would return to Harbin tomorrow. Under the hostile eyes of soldiers with fixed bayonets I gloomily transferred my luggage (quite a heavy job). Then I rumbled slowly back to Vladivostok, another 7 hours. I got a man to buy me some bread, but otherwise nothing to eat or drink. My only consolations were Rebecca West's *The Harsh Voice* (my God, I was grateful to her)

[1] I had got rid of my remaining Russian currency, which was valueless outside the U.S.S.R.

and a grumble to a sympathetic general of cavalry who undertook to get the Narkomendal [the Commissariat of Foreign Affairs] to chase Intourist. When I got back I went straight to the Japanese Consul, who gave me beer and was so charming that the whole incident reminded me of Dr. Amyntas.[1] He came round and was very good with that swine Medvedev, who is clearly rattled. Then I had supper while a drunk Greek sailor sang incessantly, and talked to Shura, who gets only 300 roubles a month and has to sell her gold rings at Torgsin. We were both half dead with fatigue.

I slept for an hour, then caught that bloody train again. A very nice Chinese *provodnik* had looked after my luggage. At the frontier I duly had my films lashed into my armpits, and felt rather silly when the customs were charming and perfunctory. They were disarmed by *Brazilian Adventure*.[2]

The country is flat and open until the frontier, where the line climbs up through scrubbily wooded hills which continue for most of the next day. At Pogranichnaya about 40 officials of 4 [3] nationalities boarded the almost empty train. They inspected my luggage more closely

[1] See *Brazilian Adventure*.

[2] Russians are brought up to distrust foreigners but to admire culture, and I always used to travel with a copy of this inferior (but copiously illustrated) book on top of the contents of my largest suitcase. The effect on British customs and immigration officials of the discovery that they are dealing with an author is probably to enhance rather than to allay any suspicions they may entertain about him; but their Russian counterparts were often mollified, occasionally impressed and always distracted by tangible evidence that one had actually written a long and quite solid-looking book.

[3] Soviet Russian, Japanese, White Russian (employed by the Japanese) and Chinese (officials in the Japanese-controlled administration of Manchukuo).

than the Russians had, and incidentally found *8 tins* of tobacco which I never knew I had. A bullying White Russian took down some particulars of me, very haphazard, then before he had finished a really silly little Japanese with rudimentary English took me to get a visa. We walked a mile uphill through a blizzard while he asked idiotic and irrelevant questions like, what was my salary? He was greatly confused by my saying that my nationality was British; he hadn't heard of it. We got to the police station, where among sub-machine-guns and fingerprints I sat and dripped melting snow while another fool took more particulars. Long before he had finished I was whisked away through more snowdrifts to the Foreign Office, where a reasonable Chinese gave me a visa and some propaganda, containing among other things the following sentence:

"Foreigners entering or passing through Manchukuo will find the new system of granting visas quite simplified and convenient."

Then I sloshed back to the station and had a huge meal of meat and vodka and told a Red Russian where his country got off and carried my luggage on to the train and slept between sheets.

[Note.—It would perhaps be wise to summarise briefly the state of affairs at that time prevailing in Manchuria, the territory in which I now found myself. The Japanese had invaded and overrun Manchuria in 1931, *the local warlords and the League of Nations offering almost equally ineffective resistance. The ultimate aim of the conquerors—not revealed until after the attack on Pearl Harbour in* 1941—*was the subjugation of all Asia; but at this stage* (1934) *they were concerned mainly to establish a ruthless and effective control over their large Manchurian*

bridgehead on the mainland. They were also anxious—partly from a desire to mask the trend of their course as aggressors, but more immediately (I suspect) because of a hankering after respectability on an international level—to garb their conquest in the trappings of a liberation. To this end they went through the usual clumsy pretence that Manchuria was an independent state. They renamed it Manchukuo (the Country of the Manchus) and installed as Emperor a pleasant, ineffective young man (Pu Yi) who was in fact the heir to the Manchu dynasty which had been overthrown by the Chinese Revolution in 1912.

In these circumstances—as I think will appear—there was an element of duality in the way the Japanese treated a traveller. They wanted him to be favourably impressed by what he saw on the surface; but they were almost equally anxious that he should see nothing below the surface. Since Manchuria is a very large country, and since most of the Japanese serving there, whether in military or civil appointments, were very stupid men, these twin aims were not in practice at all easy to reconcile.]

NOVEMBER 3

It really does feel like a different world. There is actually *lavatory paper* on this train, my first since the Caucasus, and everything is clean and unshoddy. We grope our way cautiously through the mountains, which are white and lovely in the sunshine; there are guards on the train and in front another small train containing troops and pushing a couple of empty trucks to break its fall in case of derailment [by bandits]. Boys sell pheasants at the stations, and long skeins of geese are flying east, very high up. A furry, ragged local guard turned out to welcome a Japanese officer. You see pheasants in the snow. The train doesn't go by night.

TO VLADIVOSTOK

NOVEMBER 4 (Hotel Moderne, Harbin)

Last night we stopped rather late in a small station. While I was eating I was interviewed by a fat, slug-like journalist from a White Russian paper in Harbin, much to the annoyance of my stable-mate, a Soviet consular official. The journalist told me of two refugees who had slipped across the border, and today I saw one of them, a Christ-like twitching man who has promised to come to my hotel tomorrow but probably won't.

About an hour before sunset the guard train stopped and firing broke out. There were said to be 200 mounted bandits but I never saw them. I scuttled along the exposed side of the train, enjoying it a good deal, and got some photographs of Japanese soldiers firing from under the wheels.[1] At the next station there was an armoured train, the front and back trucks being empty cars fortified with sleepers. Got to Harbin about 6.

NOVEMBER 5

Weather sunny and brisk. The noise and the character in the streets were refreshing after Russia. Spent the morning getting money, seeing Radvan (who seemed a little frigid), getting a pass from Kanai (who is an honest man, talks no nonsense, and refused to answer an innocent question about railways in the north), and lunching with G. at the Consulate-General. Here was a missionary called Overs (I bet they were maiden overs) who obscured the issues a bit but was splendidly dim-Varsity in manner. G. more withdrawn and wintry-bitter than ever, but very nice and sound, though rabidly anti-Jap. Says they squeeze.

[1] See photograph opposite p. 112.

121

After lunch we walked back to the hotel and for two hours interviewed the refugee Baranoff. He rehearsed with some intelligence the back history of the collective farm, then damned it. When peasants heard it was coming they sold their livestock, at least some of them did. When the Government found that the livestock left for confiscation were not enough for their purposes they clapped the sellers into camps. The Government issued a plan but not all the means to fulfill it, so by making up their quota the peasants left themselves with no food at all. There was much starvation and some cannibalism. A worker's winter (Sept.–Mar.) rations were 58 kgs. of beans and 12 kopeks a day. Communists—3 or 4 head men—did better, though not well. Baranoff was one of a family of 4 brothers. The father got a long sentence for no good reason. One brother and an uncle escaped to Harbin. He himself had various sentences—2 years odd in prison, and most of the rest of the time in camps. Got across the frontier inch by inch, then swam at dawn. Many patrols. In 1932 (?) there were enough aeroplanes in Habarovsk to take up at the same time 3,000 *kolhoz* delegates. Spassk is the air headquarters, with Bolshoi Mikhailovo as a station (without hangars) for summer use; B.M. is 7 km. north of Nikolsk, then 4 km. west of the line. Next most important is Botchkarevo, then Habarovsk. The frontier is said to be fortified from Hanka south. There are 150 tanks in Habarovsk, more in Nikolsk, and still more at Dauriya. No possibility of a counter-revolution, if only because they split them up so well.

I gave him 10 dollars but could not do much more that was relevant. He has had the hell of a time. Perhaps G. can help. Then I was interviewed by a Red journalist, to whom I told nothing and who took down only what he wanted and asked if I minded it coming out a little less sardonic. Then the mysterious Goldberg claimed me for a secret cabal with two local Jews, who wanted me to use my influence to get *Nash Put*, the White Fascist paper, suppressed for its anti-Semitism. I was noncommittal and left on foot for the Bank mess to dine with Monaghan. But a White journalist, an officer under Kolchak, sprang out of the shadows and interviewed me as I walked. He was a nice chap from the *Harbinski Vremya*, run by the Japs with better pay than the other White papers. At the mess I read some papers and had the usual pleasant China Coast dinner, talking too much.

Typical Harbin day, with rumours and intrigue. I had a wire from Kini Maillart [1] to say she was arriving next day, so put off departure.

NOVEMBER 6

Kini suddenly appeared by plane and we dined and went to the Fantasia and had a laugh. I talked like hell. In the afternoon G. came round and in the café where we had coffee there were more echoes of Jap blackmail. G. is too fanatically anti-Jap; an interesting case, just going to retire and not liking the prospect of England.

[1] Readers (if any survive) of *News from Tartary* will remember that Mlle Ella Maillart, a Swiss girl of unusual enterprise, was at this time acting as the special correspondent in the Far East of a Paris newspaper. I had met her briefly in London earlier in 1934. In the following year we travelled together across country from China to India, through Chinese Turkestan.

A FORGOTTEN JOURNEY

Took the morning train to Mukden. A little dreary snow at Hsinking. A foolish missionary on the train, blithering about the Oxford Groups which are now strong in Manchuria, and giving me the lowdown on Russia. Also one Wolter, a German who was beaten up by the Japs last summer and is very bitter about it. Also a White Russian with a power station up the Chinese Eastern Railway from which he is being evicted by the Japs. Also the ashes of (I think) a Japanese officer in a little box which stood on a table by the window before two wreaths of silver paper flowers on stands and was bowed to by cold mourners, mostly dressed in white, at Hsinking. Sentries stood behind it.

Got to Mukden late. Next day got my mail and with it an offer from Garvin to edit the *Observer*.[1] Respectability ho? It seems remote and irrelevant, though flattering. I shall wait for details. The rest of the days I worked on some appallingly thin articles for *The Times* at high pressure and got a lot of squash, defeating all comers including Hadland who had once been a master at Durnford [my private school], and rode beyond Pei

[1] The cable containing this offer was actually from my mother but had been dispatched at Garvin's instance. The proposal (as far as I can remember) was that I should work under Garvin for two years and then succeed him. My mind at this time was set on attempting the overland journey from China to India, and I eventually replied to the effect that until I had either failed or succeeded in this enterprise I could not give a decision. When I got back to London a year later I took no action in the matter, assuming that if Garvin still wanted me he would send for me; and he, assuming that if I was still interested I would come and see him; took no action either. So the project foundered, almost without trace.

Ling and was kindly treated by the nice Butlers [1] and got asked to Tokyo by Sansom and coined epigrams about the astonishing Walters and attended constipated press conferences and heard of Jap Moslem doings and railways towards the west and joined in grumbles about the oil racket and was treated cautiously as a celebrity and liked a man called Smith and felt Hachiya's coldness and ignored a mass of fan mail and went down perhaps badly, perhaps well, and at last got the articles done and fled to Hsinking in a boiling train.

Lovely highly-strung weather. Everyone anti-Jap.

[1] Mr. (later Sir Paul) Butler was at this time Consul-General in Mukden. On this, as on a previous journey, I received much kindness from him and his family.

FIFTH STAGE

TO THE MONGOLS

TO THE MONGOLS

———————

[*The Mongols—under Genghiz Khan a power to reckon with throughout and beyond Asia—were in* 1934 *important mainly as the landlords of an extensive battlefield. Outer Mongolia, a million square miles in area but sparsely populated, had been a nominally independent satellite of the U.S.S.R. since the end of the Russian Civil War. The Mongols of Manchuria, whose territory lies along the north-eastern frontier of Outer Mongolia, were regarded by the Japanese (in, I think, a rather woolly way) as a potential focus of Pan-Mongolian unity. A successful movement of this kind might, theoretically, have detached Outer Mongolia from Russia, or anyhow disaffected the inhabitants; and it might also have paid dividends in Inner Mongolia, which was still an integral part of China and whose rolling plateaux had in the past provided China's conquerors with their normal avenue of approach.*

I went to Inner Mongolia shortly after the last events recorded in this diary; but, although the journey yielded a series of dispatches to The Times, *the details of it are lost. I wrote down everything that happened; but I wrote it down in pencil in a loose-leaf notebook which I carried in my saddlebags, and it was all (as I later discovered) converted into a grey, indecipherable blur by the motion of the pony.*

Whether sufficient attention is paid to small, practical matters of this kind at the institutions where they teach people to be journalists I do not know.

The entries which follow deal only with the Mongols of Manchuria.]

NOVEMBER 14

Stifling rain. The usual Hsinking day with Miyakawa (Harvard; underpaid, disillusioned; friend of Ku, now in Peking). Called on Yoda, director of Mongolian affairs; charming but not informative. Poohpoohed autonomy. Building everywhere, but the Emperor's palace is not begun, though the Jap ambassador has a new house and huge offices abound. Rather well done on the whole. Dozens of droshkies and the purring cars of Japanese. Business men low type. All hate Hsinking. Lunched heavily with Tsutsui, Tsurumi (very sticky and full of childish propaganda), and Matsusomething. Also present Balet, French correspondent in Russo-Japanese war and a great character; speaks fluent Japanese.

Interviewed Hayashi, ill-informed major at headquarters who overrated my credulity. Said there were 40,000 bandits. Said Japan had only 3 divisions of 40,000 men, plus Manchukuo 90,000. Latter don't seem to be being re-equipped. About one-fifth new men. Improving fast. Then saw a man at the Opium Monopoly Bureau who was much better and poured out stuff about opium for 2 hours. I have it all down somewhere. It is a pretty racket. Then a long talk to the intelligent and charming Tani. Japan's aims nebulous but of course beneficent. Emperor helps to save China's face. Relations subterraneously improving. Very nice chap.

Straight out of this into an interminable geisha party. Hayashi drunk. Balet memorably Gallic (*Enfin, cette position n'est pas humaine.*)[1] Terrific crack with Balet

[1] Europeans never like squatting cross-legged on the floor, which is the normal practice at Japanese parties.

while a rat ran round the Yamato smoking-room. No war yet. No faith in Russians. God, how he talked. But very well.

NOVEMBER 15

Train to Harbin dawdled through a golden land laced with silver rivers under a blue sky. Grand season. Had to fill up an enormous form at the station and hear the Jap police have been after me daily at the hotel. Got my photographs, some very good. Last night Tsutsui told me, when only slightly in his cups, about a light railway south of Suifenho. I wonder why? [1] Dined rather sleepily with G., who somehow becomes less impressive and rather old-womanish. Kini wires to say she is stuck on the eastern line till Sunday. Hell and blast.

NOVEMBER 16

Got some money and saw the amiable but uninformative Angus at the Produce Export Co. Heavenly day. Carters putting their ponies into a gallop. Towering Russian horses with a horribly arch little bow on their foreheads stepping high with the droshkies, from one of which a raving beauty grins and offers me a lift. G. took me for a walk along the lovely sunset river with a huge, fabulous Englishman called, I think, Bert Burrows. He had been in the Chaco and found it lurid. At his best on vampire bats and the passions of the Russian family with whom he lodges. Ordered a pair of breeches and spent some time telephoning to the inaudible Kini at Hailin. She seems to be having a bad time.

[1] We shall never know what, if anything, underlay this pregnant speculation.

Dined on rather too much vodka with Andrew the Greek, out of Sutton's book.[1] A very *simpatico* and quite fantastic man with considerable perception. Claims to have written up in a Siberian lavatory, "Why don't you learn how to shit before you start teaching the rest of the world how to live?" This I find pertinent and witty.[2] He is the biggest talker since Balet but I like him.

This hotel is depressing. The men on the desk are devoted to me, vaguely, I suppose, suspecting that I may one day ventilate their obscure and unnumbered grievances. The café, in which the fattening waitresses move with a sophisticated air, fills with Russian Jews, pouched and paunched and faded, dressed for a vanished and shoddy Riviera. In the dank and dark red lounge harridans and conspirators keep sibilant appointments with a bilious air of disgruntlement.

NOVEMBER 17

Another no-sided long-distance conversation with Kini. Tumanov, a young detective in the opium bureau, was nice and we spent the morning in a den where the thick, handsome opium pipes were in keen demand. No test for addicts, and a licence only necessary if you want to smoke at home, when they give you a ring for your pipe and a book for purchases. Much opium bought below 1.70 [local dollars] from illicit districts. No real suppression. Bureau said to make

[1] One-Armed Sutton, a raffish but disarming Old Etonian who was something of a legend in Manchuria, where I had met him the previous year.

[2] So would anyone with first-hand experience of sanitary arrangements in the U.S.S.R.

150,000 dollars a month. Tumanov gets 170. Koreans turn nasty, Chinese don't. Japs and Koreans in the heroin business protected by extra-territoriality. Most of the heroin comes from Germany. Den was selling best quality at 3.67—worst at about 2.

As I walked to the bank a foolish young Russian Jew came up and wanted to know whether he should go to Russia when the Chinese Eastern Railway [1] is sold. I asked him what sort of a chap he was, and when he said liberal-minded and free of speech, I told him not to go. He will forfeit his pension if he doesn't, but if he does it will be paid in paper roubles. 75% of Red employees don't want to go. Typical Harbin interlude.

Bank *comprador* said rich Chinese were clearing out, but Japs were stopping them from taking their capital and new banking law will make this harder still. Small men doing just all right. Landlords bitched. Jap officers with Manchukuo troops taking to opium. Japs bad at business. This confirmed by the charming Bryner with whom I lunched and who pines for his confiscated country house in Vladivostok. Jap partners being forced on foreign firms to get contracts. Very sound on Russia. Red guards finding their parents in the forced labour gangs. Political officers still supreme. Very good lunch at the American Bar, but Unterberger is dead. Did some time-table work with Bryner, then made a date with the distant Roerich, then met a young bearded but pukka sahib who has driven a car all through Africa and will take my dispatches back to London. In the end we had a pretty late party, dining at the American Bar and getting to bed via the Fantasia at 5 a.m. I felt no

[1] A legacy of Tsarist expansion in Manchuria which at that time was still owned by the U.S.S.R.

ill effects, having refused nourishment. I always feel
well on an empty stomach. In the American Bar was a
large party of American consulars, very dashing in their
pince-nez; an aloof but sufficiently amiable British vice-
consul and his wife, he being an ex-president of the
Oxford Union to whom no doubt I was rude in my day;[1]
one coarse Japanese getting tight on beer; one intellectual Chinese in an Edwardian stiff collar, very
ridiculous; many sordid White Russians; dashing and
beautiful girls dancing unhappily with this and that;
one young German, drunk, to whom I was unneces-
sarily tough when he invaded our table. The pukka
sahib (who has some character if not much charm)
entertained two of the girls. Mine was an *ingénue* Mae
West, very nice, who improved my Russian and
hankered to come to Mongolia.

NOVEMBER 18

After a late breakfast I was interviewed by Daddy
Brown—a shade less impressive than last year—and
Admiral Wen who may never have seen a ship but is
intelligent though typically woolly on the major issues.
Unwarrantably boosted China as a strategic factor.
Then I interminably showed the suburban but agreeable sahib my photographs; then visited Roerich, an
able bearded man very like the Tsar, who is being
attacked as a Freemason in the *Vremya*, which now I
believe gets no Jap money. Walked back. Very cold.
Jap soldiers inspecting filthy pictures in a shop with
great thoroughness and concentration. Went with

[1] The *Isis*, of which I had been editor a few years earlier, did
not at that time treat undergraduate politicians with invariable
respect.

Bryner to meet Kini. A typical Harbin man deduced that I was a correspondent; finally insisted on giving me his name, written on a piece of paper with the word "drunk" after it. The only Russian in Harbin with a sense of humour.

Kini arrived but had been beaten up by Jap soldiers on the train. We had a possibly prophetic[1] scene in the stationmaster's office (out of which Kini came very well indeed), at the end of which the Jap officer apologised and produced some sort of an excuse. Japs very solemn, Russians very garrulous. Bryner rather pessimistic. Kini in good form. Dined alone and found the following phrase in a North China paper describing a missionary gathering: "The look of incredibility on the faces of those present." Kini came in late and composed a moving account of her tribulations for the French Consul.

NOVEMBER 19

Set out for Peianchen [2] early. I discovered that I had only a South Manchurian Railway pass but got through without paying for the next 2 days. Lovely day. By the Sungari dust lying smoothly on ice, with grass coming through it, looked very odd and deceptive. The North Manchurian plain is very flat indeed. Little com-

[1] It was not difficult, as one travelled in the back parts of Manchuria, to sense in the Japanese soldiery a latent desire to ill-treat and humiliate members of the white races. I always thought that this repressed urge would break out, given a favourable opportunity; and of course in the last war it did, as thousands of prisoners and internees know to their cost.

[2] On a reconnaissance, as far as I can remember, of the strategic railways then being built by the Japanese towards the Russian frontier.

pact groves on ridge crests. In the farms they are winnowing and golden clouds jet up sharply from behind the mud walls, to vanish soon. The ponies are somehow puppy-like.

New bridges are being built to replace the presumably unsatisfactory present ones. Otherwise no doubletracking. But whole line from Peianchen to Anganchi very thoroughly equipped with roots, like telegraphs, side lines, and sidings. Redoubts by bridges fly the Rising Sun.

Got to Peianchen after dark and bluffed through without a pass. Paper lanterns, vocal droshkies, truculent furry police. Dumped luggage at a Jap hotel and wandered through the wide, slippery streets. Shutters up, no wind, footfalls. Shoddy, bright Japanese cafés. Ate *mien* in a Chinese restaurant. Everyone charming, cheerful, and tough. Every conversation a high comedy. But there was a certain atmosphere of constraint when we asked about Manchukuo. Thence to a Jap café. Silly coloured lights. Tree with paper flowers. Everyone tight. Geishas amiably enduring. Ape-like soldiers swayed about the floor in the presence of their officers. I drank a thimbleful of whisky. Convincing bottle of "Jos. Herrscher Genuine Scotch Whisky." Tasted like hell. Bottom of bottle marked "Walker's Whisky." Also 2 cups of oak-apple coffee. Bill 1 gobi [the local dollar]. Air thick with barbarism. People falling about.

Set out in the ringing moonlight for an alleged White Russian restaurant. Got into a barbed-wire zone. Suddenly shouts ahead; gradually realised they meant us. Turned (instead of shouting back) and withdrew; like fools. Told K. to go slow. Watched myself automatically trying to keep between her and a potential shot: an entirely reflex action. Feet running on the hard ground. A little black policeman and a big furred Manchukuo sentry came up out of the darkness. Latter rattled his rifle bolt, for face. I stood and beamed and said "*Ingua*" ["English"] and we were suffered to depart.

We found the Russian place, a sad den where poxy plain girls danced hopelessly before two Japanese, and when these went continued dancing, a grim routine against which they showed no signs of wishing to rebel. Admittedly there was not much else to do. Over vodka we sought to pump a Russian gone to seed but having the shadow of a certain charm. He said bandits bad in the town, few troops comparatively, Japs bloody. Took out proclamation stamped with the Imperial Eagle and signed by Kyrill,[1] whose photograph appeared as frontispiece to a pamphlet. Typically hopeless and rather drunk. Then the woman of the place told us he was a bad man, just out of prison. I, warming to her rather sinister affability, foolishly missed her statement that she had a Japanese husband and plied her with strategic questions. Second mistake that night. Kini played with a kitten. At last we went back to the hotel, where we occupied 2 clean rooms for 6 hours for 9 yen.

NOVEMBER 20

They called us late and we had a rush through great cold to the station. The plain continued as before. Mr.

[1] The Grand Duke Kyrill became, after the murder of the Tsar and his immediate family, heir to the throne of Russia. Until his death in 1938 he lived in Brittany, whence the printed manifesto that I saw must have found its way across the world to fan the pathetic embers of Monarchism among the Manchurian exiles. The Grand Duke was, incidentally, an uncle of H.R.H. the Duchess of Kent.

Shin of Butterfield & Swire told us that they still do good non-official insurance business, that Heilungchiang taxes are much higher than elsewhere; in other provinces same as before, bar the remission of a special tax; good harvest but people poor and business lousy. No double-tracking. Soldiers drunk and noisy very early. Barracks at Koshan and one other place. I rashly photographed an armoured train.

Tsitsihar at noon. Dumped luggage and walked to Mission. Huge modernistic cathedral full of bright colours, where priests in beards, black robes, and fur hats played a primitive kind of tennis in a courtyard, like an Augustus John allegory. A nice bearded German told us in French that there was more opium, also big barracks and a bridge over the Nonni 10 km. to the north. Mongols are children, Chinese big children. Bandits more desperate. Two little boys came in for permission to have teeth pulled, very charming. Then we saw the head man, who had wonderful jade presents from the Chinese. Very intelligent. Long talk in German, me standing down. Fewer troops than formerly? 120 mounted bandits playing hell. Manchukuo troops go over to them. Didn't ask us to stay; most odd.[1]

Thence walked to river on outskirts, where sun had just set. Good silent moment. West red. Bastions of city fade slowly. Lights of a barracks and reddened smoke from a big fire. Also grass fires in the plain to the west. Ice grey, black figures darting on it. All sounds very clear and pure. A dog barks. A soldier bugles well. Carts shuffle woodenly in the dust, passing a gate in the barbed wire, coming up along the high embankment out of the

[1] In China missionaries generally offer to put up the few foreign travellers who find their way to towns in the interior.

vast plain like creatures crawling out of the sea. The carters joke in low, humorous tones. Black, small strips of cloud lie across the west. A gong comes from the city, and the faint crack of whips. A Japanese temple, very compact and new, lit by electric light, stands up behind us.

We walked back and got from a half-Russian shop the name of an allegedly Chinese hotel. This, when rather cleverly found, proved to be an ex-Russian hotel run by Japanese. Endless questions and filling up of forms. Then took a droshky to a Chinese restaurant, where all were charming and we had a little good food. Japanese next door making a filthy row. Kini was induced to tell me the story of her life, a good one. I did not sleep much.

NOVEMBER 21

Woke before a flamboyant dawn and walked through the main street pricing things. Brilliant day. In this weather the smoke from houses has a kind of special quality, though God knows what it is. One shop sold ginseng and bears' feet and toads and snake-skins. Japanese influence now dominates the main shops. The ponies skid madly on the concrete, the driver turning them as he might his skis. Good few military lorries, with foolish little masked men [1] obtruding themselves. A few White Russian shops.

Went back and we had breakfast and then made for the barracks, buying a torch on the way. Everything very lovely and clear. When we got near the barracks

---

[1] The Japanese Army, though dirty in many of its habits, took elaborate precautions to safeguard health. One of these was the wearing of masks to protect the nose and throat against dust.

(which told us very little) we found or thought we found that we were being followed by a little Japanese in black. Kini proceeded to photograph tombs and in the end we sheered away. Droshkied to the station, passing the little black man on the way. Sent with some difficulty a wire and proceeded to Anganchi, an hour's journey. Here K. got into the short (and anomalous ?) ladies' queue and bought third-class tickets, while the Chinese police took great pleasure, which was shared by the crowd, in sending a bloody little Japanese to the end of the long queue. Then we ate and caught the train. Two topmost berths in a crowded compartment, alleged by K. to stink of cabbage. I saw there was an open truck, as on the eastern line, with Manchukuo guards behind the engine. In flawless Chinese I got their permission to ride on the truck and take photographs, then dashed back for K. When we came they showed us where to climb up, but a Red Russian official saw us doing this and shouted protests. This rattled the three Chinese soldiers, one of them more than the others, and he turned the day against us. A charming Manchukuo commander came up with other officials and a crowd formed and we had to crawl ignominiously down. I should have waited till the train started and then got on through the first-class compartment. Stupid.

There was nowhere to sit in our carriage, so we stayed in the dining-car and saw with relief the Hsingan hills beginning to loom, black shapes gnawing into the sunset. Finally dined off vodka and red caviar and talked like hell and then went back to sleep for a few hours on the same shelf with our feet in each other's faces.

NOVEMBER 22

Got to Hailar at 3 a.m., had some tea in the station, and took a droshky none could say where. At last with the help of another arrival we forced our way into a Russian hotel, very small and disjointed and consisting principally of a billiard table, and got a small room. I slept in my boots on the sofa for two hours, then walked round the outside of the straggling town in a grey and red dawn, putting up a blackcock under some firs and treading delicately on a frozen river. Mongols in conical hats. Everyone very dashing in furs and on ponies or carts. Shops less booth-like than in Tsitsihar. More oxen drawing carts.

Came back and we had a huge breakfast of very good bread and jam and K. mended my coat. Then we had a long and finally successful search for the Produce Export Company, where we were in the end very hospitably received by a Tartar called Debedeev, who took charge of us and was charming. We went back to the town and priced a car [1] and saw the Tartar Sokolov, a good man, and had lunch with Debedeev in our room. Then we found the Mongol Yamen [headquarters], where a very intelligent young Mongol and a very impressive middle-aged one told us that we had come to the wrong place. Great contrast between the *buguan* [senior officer] and a Chinese *buguan*. An assured aloofness, instead of the surly withdrawal of a Japanese or the effusiveness of most Chinese. We went to the police, where we, especially K., had a hectic time getting permission from Oyama to go to Gandjhur. A real fool of

[1] We were hoping to get down to the territory of the Manchurian Mongols which lies (roughly) between the Hsingan Mountains and the frontier of Outer Mongolia.

a Japanese who pretended to know English obscured every issue by not knowing it. A Chinese was better in Russian, but it wasn't till another Russian-speaking officer turned up that things really got going and we got most of what we wanted. K. very good. The Solun trip is what I would like, but I suppose it's too slapdash. On the way back we stopped at the Klub Casino and saw Chinese and poor White Russians gambling on a strange table with black dominoes, pushed to them by croupiers, while the bank presided from a shelf above. In another room there were cards.

NOVEMBER 23

Debedeev came round in the morning, we in the meantime having bought two gramophone records. We went and shopped, acquiring two magnificent *shubas* [1] and two fur hats for 30 dollars. An amusing face racket over the price, which was at last solved by throwing in a pair of gloves. Charming old woman, full of jokes about her age. We also got huge and for me uncomfortable felt boots, in a shop with a nice kitten where the man made Elizabethan jokes about the legitimacy of his child.

Then we called on the Jap consulate to try and get a rifle. Here things developed well after a cold reception and we saw the consul in his house, one Kwada interpreting. 1,500 Japs in Hailar, as against 300 two years ago (or less?). Shop and restaurant keepers. Varying reports about business. They very kindly produced a rifle, which turned out to be a pump gun with twenty-three dubious buckshot cartridges. Then Kwada, suddenly becoming wonderfully helpful, took us to Colonel Terada, Dening's friend.

[1] Fur coats of a wild and woolly type.

He was a good man, "the father of the Mongols."
We sat in his bedroom. He had a bad arm. He said
among other things that there were 3,000 Buryat émigrés; that the Daurs were much better at trade and
politics than the Mongols; that there were 30,000
Mongols of all sorts in Barga; 2 cavalry regiments
totalling 1,000 men, paid 5.80 a month as against the
Manchukuo 10, but costing 30 cents a day instead of 25
to feed because they only eat meat: that the Daurs
change their names for Chinese when they come to
town; that in Outer Mongolia only the soldiers were
getting a break, but that they were pretty vague about
discipline, and one of them had conducted him across
the frontier, warning him that when they got further
they would meet a Russian officer and he would have
to behave himself (the soldier would); that on this side
they loved soldering, were admirable scouts, but hopeless about discipline (somebody else said they found it
difficult to live in barracks after the yurts); that the
lamas were not politically minded but feared Outer
Mongolia because there was no religion there and no
place in the sun for them; that there were émigrés from
Outer Mongolia but not many because it was hard;
that two Japs had been killed, and two others taken to
Urga, seeing nothing, and then sent back; that he was
afraid of what would happen if there was Mongolian in-
dependence; that the Mongols didn't know Manchukuo
from Manchester; that the chief difference they felt up
here was that foreigners quite often visited them though
they never could before; that they paid small taxes on
their livestock; that Pu Yi [the puppet Emperor of
Manchukuo] got across especially to the Daurs, who had
Ching influence in the old days and were the spokesmen

for Mongolia; no talk of princes. And a lot more which I can't remember. K. did well in Russian. He was a charming man.

We went out to the Produce Export Company in a *telega*, a minor *kibitka* lined with sacking, and lunched with Debedeev and his kindly family at 3 o'clock. Then we rattled back into town and food was bought and Kwada turned up and took us to see Major-General Hasunuma, installed in Ma's old house where flamboyance outcropped in the pillars, and bandits' ordnance decorated the walls. H. and his staff changed back from kimonos into uniform and received us noncommittally but kindly. Big horses preferred [to local ponies]. Soldiers' amusement a problem. Outer Mongolian cavalry of doubtful quality. Cavalry going to be important here, cf. Allenby. OK about cold (we were shown portentous underclothes). A little French-speaking staff officer told us that the new barracks were nearly ready, that the soldiers were proud to serve on the frontier, that the Japs liked the Mongols better than the Chinese. I was not much good here and became too involved with a weak interpreter.

Then we went to General Nakayama, a charming poet speaking Russian who also changed from the kimono. He commands a brigade. Thought highly of the Red Army but doubted if Communism could take the place of King and Country. Daurs and Buryats unreliable characters though clever. (A Buryat commands the cavalry.) And I can't remember the rest. Went back and had some beer and rice in a Jap café, where a bicycle was being cleaned, a harmonium played, and a telephone rang incessantly. A little snow falling. Not cold.

NOVEMBER 24

Bought some meat and tobacco and started fairly early. A little snow was falling. The truck, a Chevrolet, went well, but every bump we crossed threw up a cloud of dust from the dung and coal we were carrying. At the police station we picked up a disagreeable Jap officer, rank and name never divulged, who sat in front and refused to be drawn. Debedeev said he spoke English but didn't want us to know, and when we said goodbye I caught him out. He had very poor manners.

We started off in terrific form, swathed in *shubas*, and drove south-west for about five hours through very desolate lands. A bird like a thrush followed us for a bit. On the outskirts of the town we passed a troop of Jap cavalry training.[1] We passed occasional Mongols with every variety of livestock, some in fine gay colours, and two or three irrelevant-looking *oboes* [sacred cairns]. The sun shone and it was not very cold. Once we evicted some Mongols who had (characteristically?) put up their tent in the middle of the road. Sometimes there were little frozen lakes and once or twice antelope in twos or threes, small square beasts built rather like a roe. About 3.0 we got to the military yamen at [name not recorded], the place where the Ugurda [a Mongol dignitary] is. We debussed and hung about while the Japs (there was another officer here, cat-like and more amiable) thrashed things out between them. They said we had to sleep there, but we insisted on seeing the Ugurda that night. The water had been taken out of the car, so we walked the necessary 3 km. After we had started I went back for something we had left behind and to catch up got a lift in front of a Mongol on a pony.

[1] See photograph opposite p. 144

The Ugurda, a charming Chinese-looking man with a moustache, gave us brick tea with milk and funny bits of a sort of cheesy rusk made out of milk. After being polite we left the conversation rather pointedly to the Japs, on whom we looked the while as coldly as was reasonable. This, I think, was the right game to play. The yamen was full of posters, in which the most interesting thing was the way the Rising Sun was squeezing the Manchukuo flag out of the picture. Then we walked back, the Japs staying behind to discuss us or some more serious business. We were given a coldish lodging in a good small house outside the compound, and a charming Shansi cook did what was necessary with our meat. He was getting 2 gobi a day. The Chinese building fortifications near Hailar are getting $3\frac{1}{2}$. The Shansi man sent all his money home. A rather disturbed night under several cwt. of furs.

NOVEMBER 25

Spent the morning dodging the Japs with some success. After breakfast they said they were coming with us to the Ugurda. So we told the cook (who tried to refuse 50 cents) to load the lorry, which was just outside the window of their quarters, and walked on through very cold air, past the *obo* of the night before. Before we got to the Ugurda we paid a lot of visits to lamas, whose yurts were neat and as yet unvulgarised, save for one or two unimportant trademarks. The best was a charming old man in yellow with an immensely creased face who put on his peaked, winged hat and posed.[1] We had our wooden bowls with us, and thus avoided drinking out of bowls cleaned before our eyes by the nimble tongues

[1] See photograph opposite p. 144.

of syphilitics, and then dried on sleeves on which they had blown their noses many times. The Japs ran us to ground in one of these yurts, looking (or perhaps we imagined it) a little flustered and apprehensive. We left them there and made for the Ugurda again.

He told us that his title had been changed; that there was not much difference between then and now; and other not very specific things which I can't remember save as part of the general impression of these few days. The Japs arrived, late again, when we had about finished, and we went out and took a photograph of his daughter-in-law, who was looking her best in a head-dress from which two wings curved like brackets hung down concavely on either side of her face.[1] The stones were red and green, the silver was heavy. Altogether fetching. We were about to start for Gandjhur when the nicer Japanese discovered that he had left our gun behind and the lorry was sent back for it. We fiddled about, sitting in a yurt and taking pictures of the shining and compact lamasery, till it returned. But for some reason it stopped a long way away, so that we had a long walk in furs. This looked to me like the first shot in a guerrilla war, which however never developed into anything serious. (Oh, last night I forgot the speculations as to whose name and whose letter [of introduction] would be the best to play on these officers.

Well, we got to Gandjhur, about 20 cold kilometres, and it rose out of the plain very decorative and solid-looking. Three lorries had just arrived, bringing a small and (I imagine) roving unit of (I think) cavalry-men, who seemed to be putting up a telegraph (phone?) wire, and they were carrying their gear and the poles into

[1] See photograph opposite p. 145.

147

the lamasery. We had a good deal of talk about where we could spend the night. The Ugurda had promised us a Mongol yurt and the Japs at first said there was one 7 km. away. But when it came to finding a guide it turned out that this was not so, and after trying one Mongol yurt which was over-full, we spent the night in a Chinese yurt in the East Village, kept by a charming man from Peking. This place was as clean as you could wish, with soap lying about and the inmates cleaning their teeth deafeningly at dawn. There was a landmark between the village and Gandjhur, beyond which people could not live unless they were lamas. Nor could a woman sleep in Gandjhur proper.

The Chinese were charming. I never realised how much I liked the Chinese until the Russians and the Japanese made me. One of them said that no one knew anything nowadays; the Japs had control and let out only what they wanted to let out—"like the spout of a teapot." On this frontier they are less courtly and formal than elsewhere; but they talk about money all the time, just the same.

NOVEMBER 26

Again a rather disturbed night, from which we woke to the sound of teeth being brushed and a horn sounded in the lamasery. Debedeev came and made breakfast. He has been absolutely charming. He has beautiful manners, is well liked by and known to the Mongols, and plays exactly the right demure game with the Japanese, only occasionally allowing himself to flick them (as when they wanted to stop us staying the night at some yurts, on the ground that there was no water there, whereupon he asked them what they thought the Mongols drank and cooked in). At night he tucks us up under mountains of furs and cannot on any account be lured from the draught in which he lies to a better place near the fire. On all matters of etiquette he is a gentle mentor, never too late. You may not, for instance whistle in a yurt, nor may you knock anything on the grate. He says he is 55, but he is fragile and much older, I think. He is a really sweet character.

After breakfast we went and heard the young lamas intoning their prayers, making much the same noise that I first heard in Peking 3 years ago. The lama-series were well kept and the biggest was being renovated. The lamas seem to get plenty of money, which I think is pooled; and of course many of the contributions are in kind. On the roof of one of the temples were some choughs; very odd. The pictures outside the doors were always the same— on the right going in a monkey riding on a rabbit riding on an elephant trying to get into touch with a bird in a tree. On the other side a series of pictures of a man and a cow. This is all Shamanism, of which I know nothing. The usual idols, and prayer books like oblong blocks of wood. Little boys served the intoning lamas with tea. All looked very cold. Apparently you wear red or yellow according to taste. We went the round of several yurts, in which there was No Smoking, and in one of them found or were found by a Japanese spy, a young man of 26 with a little beard and the sort of mouth which K. says I shall have. He was dressed in sort of semi-military grey clothes, with rubber-soled felt boots, and spoke English. He had a pale face. He was supposed to be studying lamaism, but kept up only a very shallow pretence about it. He had been here about three months and was staying till Feb. Before he had been in Tsitsihar, "studying the life of the Chinese." He spoke a little Mongol. The lamas treated him more or less as a joke and seemed in no doubt as to what he was. He and the police were good instances of how heavy-handed Japan can be in her subtler moments. In one yurt he suddenly pointed to the lama next to him, a young, rather Bullingdon man, and said, "This one is . . . abnormal." And so he was, being weak in the head owing to syphilis and in constant expectation of the arrival of a large army which he conceived himself to command.

We fiddled about, trying to make plans for a Mongol yurt, and at last got the chauffeur to start the lorry and ran the officers to ground in the Chinese village, where they were taking a census in the yurt of a man who evidently designed tapestries for the temples. Here after some discussion, in the middle of which, to save face, they suddenly asked me my age and K.'s, we contrived to shake them off altogether and to get permission to spend the night in some yurts near the road back to Hailar. On the point of departure I caught out the one who pretended to speak no English by shooting a question at him which he answered in that language.

We bowled off across the steppe in brilliant sunshine and found some yurts about 20 kms. away. There were four or five of them, dotted round a semicircle of carts which half enclosed a dungy open corral in which the beasts were herded at night. Camels, dogs, magpies, ponies, sheep, and a few cattle among the carts. We were very well received by the head man, a charmer with a wrinkled face called (roughly) Mache. We took our things into the biggest yurt and paid a round of calls.

One woman wore a fine headdress, another had a good green dress. There was a rather vain young lama. As it got dark you could hear the sheep and cattle coming in from the steppe, and the shouts of the men herding them, and dogs barking, and the sleepy, muffled chatter of a magpie roosting in a cart just outside the yurt. We had a meal and distributed sweets and a little vodka and cigarettes and played the gramophone, which made them look dreamy and bemused.

Now what about the yurt? [1] The circular opening in the roof was half open. By day the old man used it as a clock, confirming the findings of one's watch by a glance at the sunlight coming through it. By night stars swam in it like specks in a bowl and the moon came through and slowly scoured the yurt, finding and exalting stray objects in the darkness. The brick tea—hard earthy slabs with Chinese characters on them—was made in tall, ancient copper pots. Two gigantic and well-proportioned copper flasks hung on the wall. There were a few chests and bundles, and bits of meat hung from the ceiling. When you stood up above the level of your waist your eyes smarted, especially when the Japanese chauffeur put wood on the fire. The dung was brought in in a big basket, and made a dry, welcome rattling when poured into a wooden box near the fire. There was talk of a wolf, which came to nothing. The dogs barked when a lorry passed in the night. The old man's wife kneaded the back of his head and neck before he went to sleep. At intervals through the night he spat into the fire without raising his head. The servant woman had the most humorous face there, under a kind of informal turban, and also a taste in music. The old man dandled

[1] See photograph opposite p. 145.

a little solemn girl and I am sure enjoyed feeling patri-
archal. The Japanese brought in the seats from the car
and a box and made himself an unnecessary bed which
blocked a lot of the fire. He was cold all night. In one
of the other yurts he tried to handle the woman's head-
dress and generally showed himself an amiable bar-
barian with no tact and only very obvious curiosities.
We slept under piles of furs and kept the draughts at
bay. For a few hours we got rid of that bear-led feeling
which was expressed when I said that the only person
who had never been to Gandjhur was Bernard Shaw and
he was on his way there.

NOVEMBER 27

Outside the sheep receded like a wave, the horsemen
in their midst like bottles riding the surf. It was so cold
that the Leicas were torture to handle. Dogs of the ut-
most savagery had to be kept at bay with dung, or with
the help of women and children who thoughtfully came
and stood guard, while one relieved oneself. A herd of
camels moved slowly across one horizon. The feet of the
ponies kicked up the hoar frost off the sere grass. In
winter the Mongols move more often, because grazing
is harder to find.

I borrowed a pony, which Debedeev with his usual
solicitude warned me was very fearful, and rode it out
to where the sheep were being superintended by a small
boy on a chestnut near a frozen lake. Conversation was
limited to the word "*Sein*" ("Good"). It was a good
pony. We did a little more yurt stuff, and saw a camel
being gelded with a very small penknife. They tie the
testicles on to the hump afterwards. Sheep were also

being killed; they open the stomach, then plunge a hand in and seize the heart.

Then we got into the lorry and made for Hailar. It was very cold—afterwards alleged to have been over 30 below—but the *shubas* saved us, though not from the coal dust, which made us quite black. Towards the rather bitter end of a 4 hours' run a wolf was suddenly sighted, a very big one loping along close to the road with an air of unconcern. With fairly creditable speed considering the cold I unlimbered the pump gun and had two long shots as we jolted over the steppe in pursuit. One tickled him up, but it was too far and he made off, not at all seduced by our horn, which was blown in accordance with an old Mongolian ruse. At sunset we ran past the big barracks into Hailar, had an unsuccessful quest for a bath, and slept heavily in the Golden Horn, where the same game of billiards was still being played by indeterminate ruffians.

NOVEMBER 28

Went with Kwada to the Hsingan Police and paid for the car, which came to 50 dollars, and forced a tip on the chauffeur. Oyama seemed not very much interested, but there was an able Mongol there, head of the Special Service Bureau, whatever that is. We gathered it was something political. (The Military Mission, by the way, is more or less political too.) The Mongol was thought to be getting about 250 a month. He was much defter than the Japanese. The rest of the day we fiddled about trying to arrange for a car to the Three Rivers, but decided it would cost too much in time and money, and that we had better go back to Harbin tomorrow. I

cleaned and returned the gun, and we had a boiling
bath in a Chinese place, where the boys were amazed
at the length of our limbs, especially K.'s. Then we went
to a barn-like Russian restaurant, hoping to talk with
the German proprietor, but he was away and we had
a ghostly meal in solitude to the sound of a gramophone.

We looked in at the Atlantis, a new Japanese dancing-
place. This was a pretty slap-up affair, with a band and
modernistic fittings and a stage on which geishas periodically gesticulated. There were a lot of slightly leprous
Russian girls and as usual 80% of the Japanese were
blind drunk. (I forgot that yesterday, when we were
looking for a garage, we intruded into a room where
two soldiers were quartered. They couldn't understand
Debedeev and became truculent. I tried them in elementary Chinese and an equally truculent voice and they
came incontinently to the boil. I prepared to be kicked
and cleared for action; but they contented themselves
with kicking the door open and shouting and gesturing
and seething. The air fairly sang with hatred, which I
am sure has its roots in fear.

As we were standing outside their door a blackcock
flew over the city like a bullet, high but a lovely shot.)

NOVEMBER 29

A desultory morning. K. nearly speechless with a cold
but very cheerful. First we saw the utterly uninformative head of a White Russian organisation, who did
nothing but confirm the theory that the Russians here
are a tougher and more contented lot than in Harbin.
Then we went over, I don't know why, a Mussulman
school for Tartar children, then Sokolov came round,

then we went and saw Terada, who was more charming than ever. He said that formerly there had been 1,500 lamas at Gandjhur, now there were only 200; that the Mongols were becoming more and more alive to their shortcomings; that the eldest sons became lamas; that he expected shortly some revised form of lamaism would be introduced and that in religion was the only hope of Mongolian unity; that Manchukuo was not exercising any direct pressure on the lamas, even via public opinion and propaganda; that the Ugurda received a salary, he did not know how much, and that there were 6 officials of his status in Barga; that the Mongols saw no point in the telephone, thinking that you might just as well ride over and say what you had to say; that the new railway would not affect them much, though they would distrust it because it might bring sheep to compete with theirs; that they had no use for money; that Mongols from the south came to Barga; and some more that I shall remember in time. He sent us in a car to the Mongol barracks, the little mud fort which I had seen the first day. The soldiers seemed to me a likely lot, looking more natural and effective and less childish than the Chinese; though they seemed a little uncertain of themselves.

The barracks were cold inside. All the men stood to attention when we came in except one, who went on eating out of a bowl with the air of one who has right on his side although the next man kicked him on the bottom. Pay varies from 5.10 upwards. Some bring their own horses. All bring their own saddles, and these, a gay, outlandish assortment, were laid out on trestles in the yard. That is a good touch, Terada's I am sure. There was an officer with an aquiline nose, sloping shoulders, a curious drifting gait, and the air of a demon. He said some of them understood machine-guns. The rifles are new and I think the same as the Manchukuo rifles. The kit was quite neatly kept and the place clean. Most of the men are literate.

After that we went home and packed and left the Golden Horn, with its Japanese eternally cooking and playing the gramophone, and the dog in the next yard which has no voice left, and the appalling privy, and the old woman as garrulous as a servant in a farce, and the Caucasian host, sinister, ailing, and bloated, and the samovar and the jam and the gherkins. And the *Journal de Genève*. Debedeev took us out to the Produce Export Company and stuffed us with a kind of meat pasty covered with sour cream which is a Tartar national dish, and we said with sadness goodbye to him and his Japanese-speaking son and his large kind wife. He told us that the fortifications to the north had been built by imported Chinese, who were never allowed to leave them.

We had bought third-class berths on the train, but when it came suddenly out of the cold and the darkness a sharp and prolonged action was fought between all would-be passengers. I got wedged in a corridor. It was typically Manchukuo. A Russian woman had lost her child and was trying to get out. A Mongol family with all their possessions in sacks blocked the way completely. Japanese soldiers hectored, sucking their teeth as though with ungovernable rage. A Japanese civilian, comfortably ensconced in a compartment, was trying to get his luggage passed over the heads of the struggling throng; for no reason at all, in a kind of paroxysm, he banged an old Mongol woman over the head with the sack on her shoulder. And in the middle of it all a White Russian guard, wedged and impotent next to me, started asking me my age. We finally put our luggage in the coal cellar of the dining car and drank tea and vodka until they found us a good place in a vacant compartment. Our entry in furs into the dining car was formidable, but there was only a dry English couple to *épater*.

NOVEMBER 30

Discovered that Ohta [then Japanese Ambassador in Moscow] was on the train in a special coach, so wrote a flowery chit on *Times* notepaper and interviewed him. He was charming. I told him a good many things, being in exceptionally fine voice, and he told me nothing; except that *perhaps* he dropped a very subtle hint that the Chinese Eastern Railway sale was not as certain as all that. K. was sick with angina and a little fever. I wrote up this lousy document and we reached Harbin at 2.30. Here I found mail and more about the Garvin stuff and the following invitation, a grand antidote to nostalgia if one were needed:

"29 Dorset Square   25th September, 1934
    Nov. 1

DEAR MR. FLEMING,

The loveliest party of the winter will be on sensationally original lines! It will be the first combined premiere and ball, commencing with the first English showing of a wonderful Continental film in that charming Curzon Cinema at TEN (Tues. Dec. 11th).

157

Immediately after, all the guests go next door (under awnings) to Sunderland House for the ball and a special supper by Jackson's!

Lady Portarlington, Countess Paul Münster, Mrs. Sitwell, Lady Haddington, Lady Milbanke, Lady Stavordale, Hon. Mrs. Simon Rodney, Mrs. Rudolph de Trafford, Hon. Mrs. Loel Guiness and Lady Warrender are the Principal Hostesses of "Party Number One" as it will be called (we couldn't think of a name worthy enough!).

Of course the guest-passes (we won't call them tickets) will admit to both stages of the party.

Would you join our committee? which first meets Oct. 17th (noon) at the Curzon Cinema—there'll be later meetings if you're not back by then! (Or else be a patron and take seats.)

A memorable night in aid of Queen Charlotte's— *please* let me know your wishes *soon!*

Yours sincerely,

SEYMOUR LESLIE"

The little man from the police came round and we drew him out about his salary, which was only 45, and his chief, who was better than most of the Japanese and "ought to have been a missionary." Dined with G. and went through his despatches on the Kaspe case, a dirty racket if ever there was one.[1]

[1] A talented young pianist called Kaspe, who had been on a concert tour in Manchuria, was kidnapped by a gang of White Russians who had the protection of the Japanese police in Harbin, by whom they were employed in various forms of dirty work. The White Russians demanded a heavy ransom from Kaspe's father. The latter, a Jew, delayed his reply, hating the idea of parting

DECEMBER I

Wasted the morning waiting for Tumanov the detective, who had promised to take us round the opium dens. Met Yankovsky from N. Korea, who had some wonderful hunting photographs and was nice. Also the *Vremya* journalist, who seemed perplexed about Roerich having been run out. Also the Red railway worker, who said he was going to stay in Harbin but that 80% of the others were going back: a very vague man. The nice desk man, having applied for a rise on 40 dollars, is going after 9 years to turn porter in the hopes of earning more. The Italian consul turned up, a charming droll with an eyeglass and an inexhaustible fund of anecdotes. We bought some presents for Debedeev's family and had an enormous lunch with Bryner and his kind wife, talking till dusk about Kolchak, whose betrayal Bryner's brother, then in British uniform as a liaison officer, knew all about; and about Roerich and about Kaspe. Then K. saw the doctor and was forced to go to bed, and I wrote some letters and gave them to Lady Muriel Paget, who was going through on the express and seemed very nice and effective. She had one amusing rumour about Mme. Chiang. A local journalist turned up, a truculent and gloomy man, possibly drunk. He blamed Chambon over the Kaspe business.

---

with so much money; so the White Russians chopped off the pianist's fingers and sent them to his father through the post, one at a time. Eventually the foreign community, shocked, induced the Japanese to take some action against the kidnappers, and their hide-out was surrounded. But the pianist was murdered before they could be arrested. I cannot remember whether they were ever tried, but my impression is that the Japanese police-chief stood by them and they got off scot-free.

DECEMBER 2

Cannot remember a damn thing about this day. Lunched, I think, with the younger Bryner and his ex-actress wife and two or three rather sinister Russians. She pines for the footlights, hates Komisarjevsky, and played the Shrew. Otherwise the day is a blank.

DECEMBER 3

Left for Hsinking, reading D. Sayers with immense pleasure. One doesn't read enough in this kind of life. Matsutani on the train with a hangover, nevertheless very cheerful and courteous and reasonably frank. At Hsinking talked to Miyakawa and a young nice man from the Mongol Bureau; met Lewisohn, the very saddest of men, to whom it had been denied that the Japs were going to annex Chahar; dined with Dame Rachel Crowdy, no less. Very nice. If anything of importance came up it has been digested. Oh yes. Anti-aircraft guns at Jehol.

DECEMBER 4

Had breakfast with a vulgar man who had been on the Siberian intervention, flying, and spent many months in Russian prisons, about which he was quite good. Saw Yoda, who said that the total expenditure on Mongol salaries was 20,000 yen per district, of which there are now 34; that their greatest difficulty was the gap between the upper and lower classes or stamps of Mongols, which were in the proportions of one to three; that they approved the principles of lamaism but were going to limit the numbers of the lamas and

select the men as far as possible; that the number of
Mongol soldiers was 10,000 and that they came under
the Ministry of Defence; that from Mongols in Chahar
they had had several requests for help, but these had
been refused after careful consideration on account of
the political implications; that though there were some
locally respected men among the lamas a leader was
still wanted and might be forthcoming soon when everyone got more advanced and intelligent (he rose well to
me on this, and I was fairly fly); that there were ten
Japanese lamas as far as he knew, and that a Buddhist
organisation in Japan was sending a party over to study
the religion; that about 20% of the Mongols were
syphilitic, though many more had bad skin diseases;
that their laws were the laws of Manchukuo adapted in
accordance to Mongol tradition and administered
largely by the elders in their own courts. Miyakawa
after the interview said he wished he worked for a boss
like that.

He and I had lunch, together with the gloomy
Lewisohn. Miyakawa made a good crack on seeing a
banquet breaking up and everyone puffing their way
out from the restaurant: "Jesus, somebody's eaten on
the Government." I walked round the park and saw
a skating rink monopolised by Japanese, then met the
train, on which rather to my surprise was K. We went
for a fairly inconsequent walk, then talked to Matsutani
and Tsutsue. The former tried to prove that Manchukuo
was not a rich country. Half admitted that the army
was not in favour of recognition. The latter said that
with their immensely powerful broadcasting station
they only had 10,000 listeners, of whom only 800–900
were Chinese; that the Home Office were buying 1,000

sets and distributing them; that a licence cost 1 yen a month. Matsutani said there was nothing in the big colonisation scheme which has since however been confirmed: 200,000 farmers, 2,500,000 acres, 10 years. We dined with Tsutsue and the Crowdy, looking fantastic in our felt boots; a cross between Admiral Byrd and the Duke in Exile. K. had a great success with her, and we left her and departing into the night caught a third-class train to Ssupingkai, and thence a train with Pullman-style sleepers in the direction of Solun [another Mongol area].

DECEMBER 5

Reached Taonan early in the morning and caught another third-class train to Hwaiyuanchen. K.'s throat bad; cleared some of the infection out with cotton wool soaked in alcohol on the end of a pencil. Nothing to eat but buns. At about 1 o'clock the train stopped at a desolate and uninhabited place and we got on to a truck. It had been a hot train. One old Korean in a white robe and a clown's top hat. Read publishers' advts and gossip in the *Sunday Times*. Barracks and bridging materials at Taoan, the barracks however less important than those at Taonan, which are strong

Shared the truck with three facetious Manchukuo soldiers and drove a few kms. furiously. Out of the plain at last. Hwaimiao a pleasant frontierish village under a rolling hill, surrounded by a low wall. Learnt in pidgin Chinese from nice police we couldn't go on that day. Put up at a dirty-looking but not really dirty inn kept by a Mongol, where lodged a seedy Russian vendor of overcoats and where two quail ran up and down the window-sill pecking at the paper window. Carters slept in a pile on a kang [a heated platform on which one sleeps] in a corridor. A Jap detective helped us and got us a lift on a South Manchurian Railway lorry for the next day. Then the Mongol (from Peipiao) took us out to dinner at a place where everyone was charmingly surprised. Good food, much needed.

Then on to an opium den for the sake of K.'s throat, where she puffed manfully and I without conviction or result. Mongol offered me a girl for 4 dollars; very dexterous with the opium, torturing the shiny lump over a little flame. Paid 20 cents for one packet, about 6 pipes. Then we looked in at a theatre, where a drunk Jap soldier eyed K. with purpose. Then along dark streets, outside almost all the houses in which the Mongol made obscene and inviting gestures, to a rather nice Jap café where the Mongol got off with the proprietress. And so to bed on the kang, as usual bugless. There is an *obo*, with piles of stones running out from it starwise, on the rolling down behind the village. Up there the light was lovely. There is a deserted white lamasery, on the roof of which sit pigeons and noisy sparrows; and the ruins of another very big one. We talked to an old lama who was surprised in the act of climbing on to his roof but invited us in to his spotless house. He seemed to have a wife.

DECEMBER 6

Up at 7. The Mongol took us to the Mantetsa garage via the no less charming detective. Here in the sunshine we bought and ate large quantities of *paotze* [the Cornish pasty of Manchuria], sticky, rich and filling. Then climbed on to the truck, in which the front seat was monopolised by a Jap couple with a baby and the open body of which we shared with two Japs and one Chinese (whose ears they boxed). We drove through attractive hilly country for several hours over a vile road, seeing little besides pheasants and the railway line, which ceases to be operative about halfway. Got to Solun, a one-horse place, about midday and had *mien* and millet wine in a slightly surly eating-place. Then crashed the Yamen, via some hospitable Mongol cavalry (130–180 here?) and two detectives. Taken in charge by a very kind young man with a round head and a turned-up nose; very nervous, always on the go. He put us up in a clean large Jap house, where he lives with a charming elderly lady and a Japanese butler dressed as a butler. Free fight to stave off another meal. A large, courteous, able, Russian-speaking Daur produced as an interpreter.

It's funny how one gets used to the complications of travel, and sees nothing very intricate in the fact that when a Korean doctor is produced for K.'s throat we must communicate with him in Russian through a Mongol who translates into Chinese for the Japanese to translate to the Korean.

Cars offered for the Hsingan, everything grand and very different from the Hailar police. K. went to bed on the floor and I to drink with some Tientsin men, good scoundrels, in a Chinese place. They liked the Mongols and said "*Mei yu fadze*" [1] to Manchukuo.

DECEMBER 7

Up at 7. Breakfast off rice and Jap caviar and oddments. Car at 8. Ran out into valley after valley; bare, jagged, or somehow assertively rounded mountains— like Fengtien without the cover. Frozen rivers are white

[1] "It can't be helped," an expression very often heard in China.

ribbons with a blue centre. Carts mostly oxen. Few workers, cause winter. Some live in burrows roofed with matting and straw. Road vile, hopeless in rains. Many magpies, pheasants, one small green woodpecker. No shotguns here now. Mongols make their own? Noonish came to Jap railway post. Few shacks, few soldiers, bearded men, women neat in face of desolation. 150,000(?) men working on line. Ate curry rice. Line finished to Solun in two months? Hailun one year? No line laid west of Solun. No bridges finished or work trains running from halfway between Hwai and Solun. They claim not to have decided about the Hsingan tunnel. Highest point 1,400 metres? General impression, not regarded as anything of a key show.

Went back, stopping to photograph and for two punctures, of which the second was not mended, so limped into Solun about 5 for a meal of rice, caviar, crab, seaweed and sponge cake. Also a red-hot bath, rather full of turpentine. But the point about the day was the light. This place in the winter is as beautiful as anywhere. Under the high sun the mountains were a lively dun, patterned with chocolate by burns. The trees along the streams were shining and still, the sere grass golden. Some kind of willows thrust up red branches, silver at the base. As the sun dropped the hills turned gold and then (I am sorry to say) purple. It is a heavenly light, the light of the Golden Age.

DECEMBER 8

A somehow pastoral expedition to the Hsingan Wall, called by the people here the Ghenghis Khan Wall. Ponies were produced, and two tall Japanese chargers,

which K. refused and which were in the end ridden by
our host and a business friend, quite well but rather
showily, like small boys. The rest of the party was the
local No. 1, a beaming and gigantic Mongol in glasses
and a yellow sash who wrestled cheerfully with the Japs
from horseback, and our own Mongol, whose name is
something like Ulisu, and of whom we never really
made enough use. I had much the best of the little white
ponies, indeed much the best horse out. We climbed up
the steep hill behind the town, rode along a ridge,
dropped into a valley, crossed it and came to the Wall.
This was disappointing, only an earthwork with a dyke
behind it thrown up and as it seemed to me facing the
wrong way. I mean it looked like an earthwork.[1]

We hit it on a bend or angle, and following it for a
mile or so to the crest of a hill could see it running into
the distance without wavering. We had races on the
ponies and I burst my coat when mine bolted while I
was remounting. The Mongol No. 1 was charming. On
the way back we found on the crest of the hill overlook-
ing the town a sad clustered little picnic of Japanese,
sitting on the windy side and mournfully trying to re-
create whatever in Japan corresponds to Hampstead
Heath. Our Japs showed off before them.

When we got back we found that there was after all
no bus tomorrow but a car which we could get today, so
we changed our plans and departed in a hurry and feeling rather empty, it being now the middle of the day.
We had a long warm drive, seeing the country lousy
with pheasants and partridges and the hills for the last
time change colour, and came at last to the inn kept by

[1] A vivid and illuminating description of an ancient monument
which few foreigners have seen.

the Mongol, where the best room was taken and we got what I think was the office. It had a very hot kang and was closely surrounded by conversation. We went out and had a damn good meal, choosing the dishes from the restaurant kitchen, and being as usual visited and gazed at while eating by everyone from the *chef* up. They are nice people at that place. At the inn, however, we are not quite such a success as last time. Possibly I lost face by overtipping the Mongol last time, possibly rumour has linked us too closely with the Japanese. I don't know. One never does in this elusive country. I don't care for the boy, who looks like a young Oxford poet. Prowled the streets, looked in at a café, and went to bed on the sizzling kang.

DECEMBER 9

K. not feeling too good and a wind makes the dust dangerous for her and offensive to me and the rest of the world. I called at the police station to make certain about the train, and who should I find there but Matsui, the fat man from the Chinchow geisha party 18 months ago. We recognise each other and are genial, and afterwards he helps us in small things and shares the train to Taonan. I like him. I try to tell him that he has got thinner, which is a lie, but he says "No, I am like pig" with intense conviction and in a somehow very funny way.

Then I walk round the town, buy two of the scarves which they use for belts, and eat a huge meal. Beer costs exactly double in Japanese places and a good point can be made out of this. Then back to K., who seems better, and we try to get a meal sent in but they take too long, so we go to the bus place and board the horrible machine, which proceeds at a fierce pace and in close (literally) competition with another bus to the far-off station, behind which black and white geese are flying up from a pool. Somebody has some good, very good roe heads. The train comes and attempts to go before our luggage has arrived, but in the end all is well. K. eats buns. We pass a very big lamasery, which I in my ignorance took on the way out for a Japanese research station or what-not.

At last, only slightly pestered by the police and by one man who may or may not have been police, we reach Taonan, dump our luggage, a process which strains my Chinese to its furthest limit, and walk into the darkness and dust, pursued by importunate droshkies of which we fondly imagine that we have no need. We come at last to the new and uninteresting gate of the town, which seems to be a very big one. We have no plan and 3 hours to spend and by good luck I discover from the driver of a droshky that there are missionaries here, and he takes us to the compound, which we storm with some difficulty.

Here we are charmingly received by three French Canadian missionaries, all bearded, all youngish, all shrewd, and one of them totally silent, as though he had been sent to Coventry by the others. They give us talk and food. The youngest is dumbfounded by K., and there is a good fantastic moment when she smokes a pipe given her by the boy. We make them laugh. They think that the Chinese suffer very much. I can, alas, remember nothing specific of the talk. K. is taken away to have her throat painted by the nuns, whom she finds cheerful and attractive. Then we drive back to the station and catch a train and talk and sleep.

DECEMBER 10

We hit Ssupingkai at 6, a bad time at which to get our promised railway passes and K.'s telegram from the station-master, whose office is closed. But at last I succeed, flushing a sleepy Japanese assistant from under a table. K.'s wire denies her an interview with Pu Yi and she decides to go north to Hsingking in, I think, some dudgeon. I go south reading Wortham's *Gordon* with extreme pleasure and for some reason writing down in my notebook the following phrase: "that sort of subaqueous lucidity which the skin of men's faces has in great heat." At Mukden the Butlers take charge of me, and I must say it is grand staying for the first time for three and a half months in a place where you don't have to lock everything up all the time and where you aren't badgered by the police. No mail except some blithering fan-letters and a slightly mutilated wire from Mie [my mother].

[*Note.—The entries for the next four days consist entirely of barely comprehensible statistics dealing with opium. A dispatch to* The Times (*March* 8, 1935) *notes that, " The basis of this* (*Opium*) *law—the restriction of opium-smoking to an inevitably dwindling minority of incurable addicts—has a historical parallel in the measures taken by the Japanese in Formosa some years ago, the results of which, taken on their face value, seemed to indicate in the incurable addicts a longevity which was only less astonishing than their steadily increasing powers of consumption.*"]

TO JEHOL

TO JEHOL

DECEMBER 15

Perfunctory farewells after a short night. Arrange luggage, send for negatives, interview General Doihara,[1] at top speed. He was fat, sly, nice, noncommittal. Catch train *ventre à terre*; luggage thrown on, as to wing three-quarter. Chinese train with anchovy sauce and long menu. Due 4 hours later than Sumida said. Eat Japanese food, K. sleeps, both in form. Hills crop up. Peking carts replace droshkies. Chinchow looks familiar. Board train for Chaoyang [in Jehol], buy beer and apples. An amiable female missionary from Chaoyang shares compartment. Has much admired articles by P. Fleming in *Spectator*. Mutual embarrassment.

Mongols getting more compensation than they might from Japs for railway encroachment. She is much repelled by dirt and has a stern face when asleep. Chinese get 5 dollars for a grave disturbed. Schoolchildren dragooned to too many functions. She quite sympathises with Japs who shot a family for keeping back a rifle and scaring bandits away with it. Ineffective but kindly at Chaoyang, which we reached an hour late. Romantic rickshaw journey in the very silent moonlight.

---

[1] Frequently but misleadingly called "the Lawrence of Manchuria."

Brabantic [1] scene at BAT [British American Tobacco Company] mess. At last installed in comfort by Mr. Chow, a man of the world. Business bad, no money. I have tied the wrong keys to my suitcase sent to Peking through Shanhaikuan. Posted the right ones back through the station-master at Koupeiyingtze.

DECEMBER 16

Good Chinese breakfast with Chow. First meal since light lunch yesterday. Drove to bus station (one pagoda, one big Jap restaurant). Via Mission. Saw Mrs. B——, drawn mouth, sandy, bad with Chow. Bus starts late. Slow, uneven journey, delayed by break-downs of truck. Mountains and donkeys. Sweet cakes at one halt. Peanuts and Manchus at another. One man has a little owl in a cage. Boy holds new-born calf by its tail. All stare. Soldiers in bus friendly. Fat Jap hits Chinese for no great cause. Lovely blue at twilight. Pass long bulbous caravan of donkeys, mules, and ponies carrying cotton. Alternately sleepy and exalted. Thick with dust.

DECEMBER 17

Chifeng. Arrived last night. Rickshaws through silent cold moonlight to Catholics. Charming Chinese fathers. Converse in Latin, French, Chinese, English. Former not dropped before giving peg for article on "Benefits of a Classical Education." Heads of red deer and roe. ·22 rifle. Coffee. Room with two beds and cold stove.

---

[1] See *Othello*, Act I, Scene i:

"*Brabantio appears above at a window.*

BRAB. What is the reason of this terrible summons? What is the matter there?"

Dinner European. Opium for money, later *abrutissement*. 400 (?) dens. Weichang line difficult, because of river. 150 soldiers left for Linhsi in December. War with China?

Huge sleep, huge breakfast. Grey dusty day. BAT man fearful. Missionaries repellent. Town has wide streets, no character. Lunch and Chinese lesson. Bleak school treat to Hungshan. Climbed, children dots below us. Père Suen as agile almost as delightful. Red rock, dust obscures plain, boots and coat encumber. At foot of mountain first rock pigeons, then superb high partridges. Desolate pagoda, squalid family. Children squat round bowl of ashes. Woman forgets truculence for courtesy when given cigarettes. Family of eight peasants next door. Dirty and *décolletés*, running noses. Opium 90 cents. Farmers can't sell, keeping. Bullets in mission gate. Call at mission, black tea, uninspired cakes, foul voices. Good story re Yoshida, head of power station, warning him in Sept. not to send wife via Siberia in Nov. because war in Nov. Female missionary humanised by reference to camels. Dismal folk. Male missionary at pains to make female's presence above board. They knew nothing. Back for a bad but delightful semi-Chinese dinner with *les pères*.

DECEMBER 18

Up at 6. Huge breakfast, fond farewells. Outstripped carriers, who disappeared with our luggage. Grave loss of face by the father who had made a new key for my suitcase. They cropped up as the bus was leaving, but I lost my seat to a fat Jap, and with Kini on my knees meditated over a number of miles the advantages of travelling light. Flattish bad road, mostly along river bed; easily washed out. New road near Weichang which is dominated by a sharp peak. A long town between river and mountains, like all (?) the towns in Jehol. Big inn opposite bus station. Cold large room 80 cents, small warm room 50. But it was cold after dinner. Climbed to Taoist shrine, well received, gave 5 cents. Roofs grey and rectangular below us, very undecorative.

Country naked, beautiful. Sounds very clear. No bus tomorrow. Blast Sumida. Try Jap commander, who is powerless. Our one friend is the postmaster, who speaks a little English. Delicious dinner at inn. The warm kang room is filled with smoke. Police still don't believe we don't understand characters.[1] Mahendra Pratap[2] was here 4 or 5 days, speaking bad Chinese, taken for a missionary.

DECEMBER 18

Fried in the night [by an over-heated kang]. Lovely day under the mountains. Water frozen in our room. Walked the street. Many Jap goods. Heavy good breakfast. Walked out to wall. Heavenly bare mountains. Donkeys, man delousing. Brushwood market. Magpies,

[1] The Chinese are well accustomed to what they say not being understood, a contingency which frequently arises when they meet a compatriot from a province with a dialect radically different from their own. When this happens they (if they are literate) often sketch the character or characters making up the word which has caused a deadlock, either in the dust or with a finger on the palm of one hand; for although "cat" in the north may be pronounced "dog" in the south the ideograph is the same for both sounds. The country people believe all foreigners, however inarticulate, to be learned and are at a loss to understand why this foolproof formula fails to work with those who are not Sinologues.

[2] A down-at-heels Indian revolutionary, employed by the Japanese in connection with propaganda to the Moslems.

broad street. Tried to work in inn, too dark, cold. Finally ran down café where they were charming, but tried to play the gramophone and charged us 2.10 for cocoa, *sake*, and dried fish. Our whole bill at the inn was only 3 dollars. Went and had bath in steaming crowded place. Felt grand.

DECEMBER 19

Bus at 8 on stomachs empty save for peanuts. Good seats and smuggled luggage. Bloody driver. Second bus constantly *en panne*. A Chinese attached to it savagely beaten up by Jap with starting handle. Lovely mountain passes. Hunting boxes in firs. A little snow. New untouched road. One concrete bridge made. No work going on elsewhere. Soup at Lungwha, where there is a good yamen, bright colours, much mistletoe. Dust all day like a fog. Took streets too fast. Carts on ice. Camels. Suddenly came on Chengteh. First the club-shaped rock, then Tashi Lumpo (now fronted with Manchukuo barracks), then palace pagoda. Gave names and ages to Military Mission man, then walked through busier fuller [than on my last visit in 1933] streets to Conard,[1] who was delightful and lodged us in luxury. The sad Lewisohn also there, leaving tomorrow. In clover, but police on our trail.

DECEMBER 20

Called headquarters, told to come back at 1 p.m., raced to temples, climbed hill in full regalia, saw Potala. Two lamas there said Manchukuo was good,

[1] There can be few travellers who have visited Jehol and who do not remember Père Conard, a shrewd and hospitable Belgian, with gratitude and affection.

Peking would soon be Manchukuo, Dolonnor was Manchukuo, there were 200–300 lamas in temples, had been
one Jap, were 3 at Dolonnor. Tried to sell us scraps.
All the old birds, plus a raven. This really is fairyland.
Ran back sweating to headquarters, saw Kaido, had
success. Started Wangtao,[1] got on to roads and con-
servancy problem, tried the western frontier, made him
angry. At last he said it needed rectifying near Kuiyuan.
Blamed Chinese for vague frontier. Enthusiastic about
Mongols. At present less well trained than Manchukuo
troops, but very brave, would be good army, he would
like to lead them. No Mongol troops in Jehol. Warmed
to question about amusing the Jap soldiers, said they
were hunting rabbits. Won him over, I think.

Interpreter (Manchukuo language officer) took us
over the park. Much as before but slightly raddled.
Military hospital. Deer shyer. Interpreter said our
questions had been audacious, thought I knew a lot.
Moving divisions expensive but now cheaper. Thence
rickshaws to Opium Monopoly Bureau. Nice unofficial
lot of Japs. Said doubtfully that 1,200,000 dollars of tax
went to local government. Bought at 1.70. No licences.
Took us to one official den. No one there, not even
heated. Then another small place. Kang for five. Took
5 dollars a day. Sold one tablet for 10 cents. 35 tablets
to a *liang*, which they bought from Bureau for 2.20.
After dinner (which by this time we needed) hit up
two cafés. One was the Gaika where I brawled last
year. Much modernised. Silly conversation with the
golden-toothed geishas. "How many years you?"
"Twenty." "And you?" "Eighteen." "And you?"

---

[1] Wangtao, "the Princely Way," was a bogus sort of philosophy
on which life in Manchukuo was supposed to be based.

"Ten yen." In the other café (a new one) a Korean girl from Tientsin found life hard and a drunk chauffeur did his best to make friends.

DECEMBER 21

Shao, head of Ind. Dept.,[1] called at 10. Fat, intelligent, good Manchu. Needed an innocent questionnaire to take away for Japs' benefit. Afforesting at officials' expense; poplars and pines. Cotton. Had warned Terada against favouring young Mongols too much at expense of priests (princes ?). Conditions in country appreciated by people but not in town because no business.

Called on the Merry Widow [a Chinese gentlewoman]. Huge house, only two rooms left to her; husband, brilliant man, died with Jap boots clumping past his window. No payment for billets. Latrines in big garden. Baby grandson forgot himself on kang, deftly gathered away bottom upwards. Pears from her garden. Apelike Jap soldiers in evidence. After lunch K. went to temples, I to Ando, nice but noncommittal. Customs frontier extends to Great Wall. Has a man "studying conditions" in Dolonnor, which lorries can reach in one day from Weichang if rivers are frozen. Renewed impression of vague frontier. Thence uphill to missionaries, both dim and mouselike; Mrs. Panter at tea with them but all went well. All pro-Jap, ill-informed. Peasants all grow cabbages after opium. Road workers well paid, lightly worked. In offices many Chinese replaced by Japs.

Back to Conard's, badgered by gendarmes who stayed an hour. Asked among other things what was

---

[1] I have no idea what this was.

the chief difference between now and my last visit in June last year. I said that now it was very, very much colder.

Dined with Shao, good food, ate a lot. He would seem to be an idealist. Good future for sheep in Barga. Manchus pleased with Pu Yi. And what else?

TO PEKING AND POINTS SOUTH

TO PEKING AND POINTS SOUTH

DECEMBER 22

Up at 5, after long pleasant talk with Conard last night. Chinese won't stand for rapine from bandits. Lin Kwei-tang brought from Shantung by Japs; affair of his adjutant and telegram. 100 girl boxers *v.* 18 Russian soldiers.[1] Three Americans to Dolonnor. Walked to truck. Started for Peking 6.30, dark, passed long convoy of carts with three Jap cavalrymen. Grey Scots morning. More comfortable than bus. Climbed several passes tortuously. Road not too bad.

At noon reached Kupeikou, whence the Great Wall goes staggering away over the hills. Only a few towers damaged [in the fighting in 1933]. Manœuvres going on in river bed. I photographed Lewis-gun section and other things while K., guessing, sought to distract by taking innocent photographs in the street. Soldier told me not to, but we smiled and he was ignored. Then bloody Jap in Chinese dress got a gendarme and arrested me. Taken to head-quarters. Messengers sent for interpreters. I got in touch with K. and she, under close observation, got my unused film out of the lorry and palmed it to me.[2] But alas we bogged it and it

[1] This sounds interesting, but alas, time has expunged the details of the contest from my memory.

[2] So that I could substitute it for the exposed film if the Japanese ordered me to hand over the latter.

dropped on the floor. Still they suspected nothing. Rattled the little civilian interpreter with many questions, particularly about lunch, which by then we needed. Finally released after being asked what we thought of Manchukuo. Given lunch by the Foreign Affairs Dept. in a Jap place. Bag (this is irrelevant) 53 snipe, 12 pheasants, 18 quail, 1 duck, 1 dove.[1]

K. gave them hell for not producing Chinese food. Senior Chinese was charming, two Japs quite nice.

The truck hooted impotently outside. Finally we got on and went through the perfunctory Chinese customs, one passenger beaming because I imagine he had got some opium through. The road got much worse and a following wind gave us hell with the dust. Very long journey, 12 hours altogether, through Miyun. The Wall followed us for a bit, careering over the hills. Some slow-flying herons. Sleep on a bench. Very tired. Hit Peking after 6. Truck left us outside the north gate. Got in, a long drive in rickshaws, showing cards to police, who were a great contrast to the Manchukuo variety. Sensation [2] at Wagons Lits Hotel, where a Swiss ministered to our complicated needs, which were chiefly to telephone after our luggage, which finally turned up minus the keys very late. Meanwhile I had got my boring mail and a visit from Harding [of the British Legation staff] and Macdonald [*Times* correspondent in Peking] and a fan letter from one who had seen my name in the visitors' book. Macdonald seemed sound

[1] This unusually inconsequent entry must have been made when I was typing arrears in the diary on board a houseboat on the Yangtse, a few days later.

[2] Owing to our outlandish and dirty appearance.

on Mongolia, but I didn't on an empty stomach take much in. Very late got a little food and slept.

DECEMBER 23

Up early, feeling rather worn. Plane at 11. Had been held up on flight north and cannot make Shanghai today. Neat chess-like parade going on as we took off. Soldiers in barracks waved bugles at us. My Leica sealed up; detached seal without difficulty. Dull flight over plain, along saltings on coast. Fat, repellent, likeable American doctor on board, trying to catch boat from Shanghai at 9 tomorrow. Got some peanuts to eat at Tsingtao. Thereafter a few mountains. Landed at Haichow towards dusk. Some confusion. Wire had not arrived. Roads impassable on account of mud. Mission inaccessible for the same reason. Two charming, handsome American pilots and the passengers finally went off to a private Chinese hotel in Sinpo (?). Damn comfortable, though it appalled the others. Grand dinner, with raw food being cooked in a boiling dish and good wine, locally made. Talked too much to the local APC [Asiatic Petroleum Company] Chinese, a man of great intelligence. At Haichow is the beginning of the Lunghai railway.

DECEMBER 24

Up at 4.30. Rickshaws out to the plane, which squatted in mud guarded by ragged soldiers with very new Mausers. Took off before 6, before it was light, after carefully reconnoitring the runway. As the light grew in the east the land looked very queer, like a kind

of modernistic window, on account of the neatly parti-
tioned expanses of water. Crossed the Yangtse and landed
Shanghai about 8.30, the doctor dashing off to catch his
boat. Clouds and mud a great contrast to the north.

DECEMBER 24–31

Tony and John[1] as nice as ever. On Christmas Eve we
went out to Minghong, passing on the way a man who
was to have joined forces with us up river and whose car
had overturned. One dog killed, one wife shaken.
Chugged upstream, talking like hell. Moored alongside
Merganser and Feng Hwang [two other houseboats].
Dined on one of them with the A——s (she a Gaiety
girl, he sad and not liking her; Maugham wrote *East of
Suez* about them) and the B——s, he Welsh, fond of
shooting, she non-speak. Next day started off well at a
clump of high reeds. With my first four shots got a cock
pheasant and three snipe, two of them a memorable
driven right and left, both dead in the air together and
falling within three feet of each other. Then we marched
and counter-marched with fair success, came back to
the boats for too much lunch, then the Keswicks and I
went out to try and flight the duck. I got one down but
could not pick it in the dark. Stood over my knees in
mud for an hour and a half. Bells from a Catholic
mission in the village the sole reminder of Christmas.
Another gigantic meal and so to our bunks.

Boxing day a longish walk. At one time we got into a

[1] Tony and John Keswick, whose grandfather founded the firm
of Jardine, Matheson & Co., were old friends. On this, as on
previous and subsequent journeys, I had good reason to be grateful
for their kindness and their counsel.

lot of snipe and I got a screamer. Then the most curious and acute gun-headache intervened, and I had to relapse on to a tomb until it had passed. After that the best bit was a bog-hole where John got three high snipe and I one. Returned through waterish village. Total bag: 53 snipe, 12 pheasants, 18 quail, 1 duck. A lot of good jokes and a grand Christmas. Those two couldn't be nicer.

In Shanghai I saw a lot of people but what they said I can't remember much. Eventually flew to Nanking in a bum seaplane, which departed into a rainy Sunday morning carrying Tony onwards to Hankow. Rupert S. was charming and we talked and drank for some reason eggs in sherry and then I fell into a deep sleep, being very tired. Dined with the majestic Blunt and Chiung, ex-Vice-Minister of Justice, a great Johnsonian. Said Johnson's outlook partly Chinese, e.g. crack about dining with a duke.[1] Talked very slowly and rather drunkenly, or he would have been interesting. I showed off a bit. Then caught train, and here [2] we are in the north again and they tell me it is New Year's Day and I wish to God I had had time to take notes in

[1] "BOSWELL: I said, I considered distinction of rank to be of so much importance in civilised society, that if I were asked on the same day to dine with the first Duke in England, and with the first man in Britain for genius, I should hesitate which to prefer.

"JOHNSON: 'To be sure, Sir, if you were to dine only once, and it were never to be known where you dined, you would choose rather to dine with the first man for genius; but to gain most respect, you should dine with the first Duke in England. For nine people in ten that you meet with, would have a higher opinion of you for having dined with a Duke; and the great genius himself would receive you better, because you had been with the great Duke.'"

[2] In Peking, presumably.

Shanghai. Very glad to be back in a clean and frosty land.

1935

JANUARY 1-5

Rather desultory day. Saw the Soviet Bittner, who forked out £26 from Vladivostok [1] and ingenuously tried to pump me about Jehol. Met the Owen Lattimores, who are particularly charming and were nice to me. Oberg, a one-eyed Swede, came in and a trip was provisionally arranged to Kweihwua; this decided me to leave at once for Tokyo and get that over. Saw Macdonald and dined with Behrens and Harding. The latter went to sleep and the former seemed to me to have got almost everything the wrong way round. Got some American reviews [of *One's Company*], one of which gave me hell in a rather intelligent way. Spent most of the next day staging my getaway. Talked to the nice Cadogan [Sir Alexander Cadogan, then H.M. Minister in China], who seemed sensible. Was interviewed by a literal-minded girl. Lunched with the Cadogans, where Kini was. Wrote to Geoffrey Dawson and dined with K. in an amusing German place at her hotel.

Next day saw Roerich, who told me how he was run out of Harbin. In the middle the Soviet money was delivered to me, intriguing him a good deal. Saw Norin, the best man so far, who made me hopeful about the

[1] A refund rather surprisingly produced by Intourist in Moscow as a result of my complaints about my treatment by their branch in Vladivostok and handed over by Bittner, who was Councillor in the Russian Legation.

Kokonor[1] and has a Russian expert on tap in Tientsin.[2] I think we got on well. Lunched with Holman, Behrens, and Denzil Clarke. The usual pleasant Legation atmosphere. Squash afterwards. Holman was no good and just about passed out after three games. Clarke was much better and should have beaten me but I just won. Had an egg nog with the Clubbs, he very Americanly an expert on Communism. Then saw Giles Hall and some others at the Club, then picked up K. and we had a grand dinner with the Lattimores, Turkestan food served by the famed Moses. Some form of Countess who was present had been in a railway accident in Russia and grumbled that that man Fleming capitalised his, why couldn't she? I am no good at these sort of moments and look either haughty or apoplectic with embarrassment. K. and I stayed late, talking like hell and liking the Lattimores immensely.

Next day I caught a train to Shanhaikuan, talking to a French bookseller as far as Tientsin and after that having absolutely nothing to do. At Shanhaikuan I collected a pass forwarded by Sumida, then went to see C——. It was well worth it. On his door was written in English and Chinese "No Man's House" (his Christian name is Norman), and for a long time it was impossible to force an entry. At last I got in and the boy roused C——, who was not only asleep but drunk, after a naval lunch.

He looked rather like the cartoons of Little Willy, raffish yet ineffectual. "Make yourself at home," he said, and gave me some photograph albums containing many pictures of dogs, many pictures of C——, and

[1] See photograph opposite p. 177.
[2] This refers to plans for an overland journey to India.

some memorable suburban pierrettes. Then he took me out to dinner with P—— of the Customs, but after we had walked for a long way it turned out he was engineering a call on the Japanese Military Mission. The head of it was away, so we had to go round to his adjutant, who didn't want to see us in the least, but spoke of an independent North China. "That man is an orphan," said C——, "and I have adopted him." He also said he had been scapegoated by the Chinese Government. Whenever he said "we" he meant the Japanese. He gave me a lot of silly propaganda in a portentous way and got lost looking for P——'s house. At last a policeman found it for us, an ex-missionary place containing P——, a brave man going to seed, his Jap wife from Shanghai, shoddy but very nice, and a Jap guest who vanished at once. Here I got a little food, my first since breakfast, and ran C—— back through the streets, while he kept on telling me that he was an officer and a gentleman. He has pictures of the Prince of Wales and Mrs. Roosevelt in his room. We passed a place labelled "Japanese Restaurant. First Class Whore House" and another "No. 1 Japanese Girls." Said to be inspected twice a week by an army doctor. At the train he lost face because the Jap passport people were maddening. A wonderful man.

Spent an hour after we started fixing up some trouble over a German passenger's ticket. My technique finally triumphant. I must be getting rather good. Arrived Mukden next morning, breakfast with the Butlers, a haircut, a railway pass from Sumida, some books; snow on the ground. Now running towards the Korean frontier through shining hills.

This is the last page of my diary.

THE END